Thomas Jefferson's
COOK BOOK

Thomas Jefferson's
COOK BOOK

Marie Kimball

Drawings by Cinder Stanton

University of Virginia Press
Charlottesville

First paperback edition published 2003
ISBN 0-8139-2214-3

3   5   7   9   8   6   4   2

Contents

Thomas Jefferson...
Gourmet

"Thomas Jefferson," said his political rival, Patrick Henry, "came home from France so Frenchified that he abjured his native victuals."

Like many of the "unbounded calumnies" heaped upon him by political enemies and certain Federalists, this was not true. Long before he went there as minister plenipotentiary, he had imported French delicacies and wines for his table, and he had cultivated at Shadwell and Monticello a large variety of vegetables, fruits, and garden stuffs not commonly grown on the smaller Virginia plantations.

Jefferson retained his fondness for such native staples as sweet potatoes, corn, black-eyed peas, turnip greens, shad, Virginia ham, venison, wild swan, crab, scuppernong wine and grapes, throughout his life. In France he delighted guests by serving Indian corn on the cob which he had grown in his Paris garden. He had merely added to an already cultivated palate a taste for some of the finer nuances of French cookery.

In the matter of wines he was accepted among his friends as the ultimate authority. For President George

Washington he selected and ordered 65 dozen bottles of wine in 1790; and when his friend James Monroe was elected in 1818 to the "splendid misery" of the presidency, the former president devoted all but six lines of his letter of congratulation to a disquisition on the best wines for official entertaining.

Being a methodical person, President Jefferson took regular inventory of his fine wine cellars, and recorded that a great deal more wine, especially champagne, had to be provided when Congress was in session. He estimated his annual need for champagne at 500 bottles, calculating that after dining 651 persons, in addition to other wines, he needed 207 bottles of champagne, or a bottle for every 3 and $\frac{1}{7}$ persons. For "wine provided at Washington," in 1801 he bought "five pipes of Brazil Madeira; a pipe of Pedro Ximenes Mountain, 126 gallons, 424 bottles of it sent to Monticello; a quarter of a cask of Dent; a keg of Pacharetti doux; 400 bottles of claret; 540 bottles of Sauterne."

The gourmet of the White House regarded wine as "a necessity of life," and said that as a moralist he rejoiced at the prospect of a lowering of the import duties, because, "No nation is drunken where wine is cheap; and none sober, when the dearness of wine substitutes ardent spirits as a common beverage."

Olive oil was one of the other importations Jefferson considered a practical necessity. He was extremely anxious to establish its culture in this country. Although he had dabbled in introducing viniculture into the United States and even to nearby Colle, after he had studied the wine-producing area in Europe he wrote William Drayton of South Carolina on July 30, 1787, from Paris: "Wine too is so cheap in these countries that a labourer with us, employed in the culture of any other article, may exchange it for wine, more and better than he could raise himself. It is a resource for a country . . . whose good soil is otherwise employed, and which has still some barren spots and a surplus of population to employ on them. There the vine is good, because it is something in the place of nothing."

It was in this same letter that he asked his friend of the Charleston Agricultural Society to attempt cultivation of the olive in South Carolina, which he thought might grow in that area. Jefferson sent him a cutting of the olive of Aix, which he considered the finest for oil. "The olive," he said, "is a tree the least known in America, and yet the most worthy of being known. Of all the gifts of heaven to man, it is next to the most precious, if it be not the most precious. Perhaps it may claim a preference even to bread; because there is such an infinitude of vegetables which it renders a proper and comfortable nourishment."

As a substitute for olive oil the master of Monticello also experimented with oil made from the benne or sesame seed. The seeds had been brought by slaves from Africa and flourished in South Carolina. The seed could also be used to sprinkle on bread or small cakes.

The search for a good source of oil was linked to Jefferson's fondness for salads and vegetables. He often attributed his long life to the abundance of vegetables and salads in his diet rather than animal flesh, and to his preference for wine over strong spirits.

The kitchen garden at Monticello contained the greatest variety of vegetables, and he imported garden seeds, vines, trees and plants from Europe and from famous gardens and seedsmen in this country. Unquestionably his favorite vegetable was the pea; and his garden book records more than thirty varieties, from "the earliest pea of all" to the last on the vine at the first killing frost. And many of these were dried for winter use.

It was the custom in Albemarle, and among gentlemen gardeners, to compete for the honor of serving the first dish of green peas in the spring. Jefferson won the honor

so often from his friend and neighbor, George Divers of
Farmington, that he instructed the children to say nothing
of their having had green peas, but to allow Mr. Divers
the pleasure that year of giving the great dinner.

Other vegetables grown in profusion, and whose cultivation was carefully recorded in his Farm Book, included
broccoli, globe artichokes, sprouts, corn salad, asparagus, cabbage (in great variety), beans, cauliflower, celery,
eggplant, squash, carrots, parsnips, scallions, melongena,
salsify, tomatoes, spinach, Jerusalem artichokes, hominy
corn, potatoes, and pumpkins. From 1801 through 1808,
the President of the United States carefully noted on a
chart, "A Statement of the Vegetable market of Washington during a period of 8. years wherein the earliest &
latest appearance of each article within the whole 8. years
is noted."

Among the "garden stuffs" commonly used in salads
in Jefferson's household were cucumbers, cress, endive
(of many varieties), radishes, dozens of kinds of lettuce,
chicory, mustard greens, chives, cabbage, spinach, pep-
pergrass, asparagus, and tomatoes.

Preparation of the food in Jefferson's household was
given careful attention and scrutiny. His daughters were
carefully instructed in domestic arts along with their
lessons on the harpsichord and in Latin and Spanish. On
May 22, 1785, he employed Adrien Petit in Paris as his
maitre d'hôtel, "consequence of embezzlements and depredations committed by M. Marc, the late Controller of
Finances in his Department."

From that time on, the handwritten family cookbooks,
the food and wines served at the tables always spoke in
French without ever losing a strong Virginia accent.
There were "Blanc Mangers" made by Petit's rule or
"Chicken a la Marengo" by Annette. The spelling, too,
was polyglot but evidently understandable to the ladies
of the household who superintended a series of colored

cooks serving their apprenticeship under Petit at Philadelphia and Monticello from July 19, 1791, until he became homesick and departed for France in 1794 leaving behind a rich legacy of friendship and culinary memories.

Petit's successor Etienne Lemaire continued the tradition of his countryman and served Jefferson during the presidency. Writing to his daughter from Washington he told her, "I enclose you Lemaire's receipts. The orthography will be puzzling and amusing but the receipts are valuable." One was for "pannequaiques."

Among the memoranda left by Lemaire was one "Facon Demployer different sorte de vin à Lusage de la cuisine Francaise." Despite orthography, his wisdom became part of the culinary skill and tradition of several succeeding generations of those schooled as Jefferson's daughters had been in the fine arts of hospitality.

Mr. Jefferson's hospitable habit of "mitigating business with dinner" continued throughout his life, whether as minister to France, President, or Sage of Monticello. Abigail Adams found the entertainment offered by her husband's successor extravagant to a degree, and his administration "one long levée."

A guest at the President's house gives a fairer picture than the embittered Mrs. Adams, "Never before had such dinners been given in the President's house, nor such a variety of the finest and most costly wines. In his entertainments republican simplicity was united with epicurean delicacy; while the absence of splendor, ornament and profusion was more than compensated by the neatness, order and elegant simplicity that pervaded the whole establishment."

Helen D. Bullock

The Epicure of Monticello

"The whole of my life has been a war with my natural tastes, feelings and wishes," Thomas Jefferson remarked in wistful retrospect on his retirement from the presidency. "Domestic life and literary pursuits were my first and my latest inclinations, circumstances and not my desires led me to the path I have trod." It is not surprising, in view of this confession, to find that our first Democratic President, whom we tend to think of as occupied with such lofty thoughts and ideas as are embodied in the Declaration of Independence or the Statute of Virginia for Religious Freedom, was one of the greatest epicures and connoisseurs of the art of living, of his day. The choicest delicacies of two continents made their appearance on the presidential table, the finest wines were imported from France and Italy, the food was prepared by French chefs, and the whole was supervised by the President himself.

Jefferson had been left a widower early in life and the management of his household, as well as his plantations, fell upon him. He showed the same interest and punctiliousness in his domestic affairs as he did in those of state. The selection of a cook or a maître d'hôtel was given no less thought than the choice of a minister plenipotentiary. He penned a rule for "Nouilly à macaroni" with the gravity that he signed a treaty. It was no unusual thing for him to pause in his official duties to write his daughter: "I enclose you Lemaire's receipts. The orthography will be puzzling and amusing but the receipts are valuable." The receipt was for "pannequaiques."

When Jefferson set sail for France in 1784, as Minister Plenipotentiary to the court of Louis XVI, he was, all unwittingly, leaving behind him the Virginia tradition of ham, fried chicken, Brunswick stew, greens and batter bread. The cuisine of France was a joy and a revelation to him. During the four years he lived in Paris Jefferson devoted himself to the intricacies of French cooking. The most precious recipes of the cuisinière, whom he employed at three hundred francs a year, with an allowance of one hundred francs for wine, were carefully copied in his own hand and brought back to the United States. Thus it happens that our first American recipe for ice cream, then no vulgar commonplace, is in the writing of a President of the United States.

Although General Washington seems to have had the first ice cream freezer on record—he noted that in May, 1784, he spent "1. 13. 4 By a cream machine for Ice"— Martha Washington's numerous recipes do not include one for ice cream. Jefferson, however, made his as follows:

2 bottles of good cream
6 yolks of eggs
½ lb. of sugar
mix the yolks and sugar

put the cream on a fire in a casserole first putting in a
stick of vanilla

When near boiling take it off and pour it gently into the
mixture of eggs and sugar

Stir it well.

put it on the fire again stirring it thoroughly with a spoon
to prevent it sticking to the casserole.

When near boiling take it off and strain it through a
towel.

put it in the sorbetière (ice pail).

then set it in ice an hour before it is to be served. Put into
the ice a handful of salt

put ice all around the sorbetière
i.e. a layer of ice a layer of salt for 3 layers.

put salt on the coverlid of the sorbetière & cover the
whole with ice

leave it still half a quarter of an hour

Then turn the S.in the ice 10 min.

Open it to loosen with a spatula the ice from the inner
sides of the S.

Open it from time to time to detach the ice from the sides

When well taken (prise) stir it well with the spatula

put it in moulds, jostling it well down on the knee

then put the mould into the same bucket of ice

leave it there to the moment of serving it.

to withdraw it, immerse the mould in warm water, toss-
ing it well until it will come out & turn it into a plate.

This ice cream was served in a more elaborate way on
state occasions in a manner somewhat similar to the
"Baked Alaska" so favored during the opulent nineties.
One visitor to the White House reports that at a presidential dinner the ice cream was brought to the table in
the form of small balls, enclosed in cases of warm pastry,
a feat that caused great astonishment and murmurings.
Indeed, Jefferson's predilection for intricate dishes, usu-

ally of French origin, was at times the occasion for unfavorable comment, no matter how palatable they had proven to his guests. His great antagonist, Patrick Henry, denounced him, in a political speech, as a man who had "abjured his native victuals," and was unfaithful to good, old-fashioned roast beef.

An ice was but one of the delicacies Jefferson learned to make in France. His servants were interviewed and his friends implored to yield the secrets of the kitchen. "Biscuits de Savoye, Blanc Manger, Meringues, Macarons and Quacking Jellies" were favored eighteenth-century viands for which Jefferson diligently transcribed the recipes. Sometimes they were in English, sometimes in French, now and then partly in each. The ingenious rule for "Wine Jellies" begins gaily in English: "take 4 calves feet & wash without taking off the hoofs. These feet must be well boiled the day before they are wanted." The "Meringues," however, are thoroughly "hyphenated": "12 blanc d'oeuf, les fouettes bien fermes, 12 cueillèrres de sucre en poudre, put them by little and little into the whites of eggs, fouetter le tout ensemble, dresser les sur un papier avec un cueiller de bouche, metter les dans un four bien doux, that is to say an oven after the bread is drawn out. You may leave them there as long as you please."

After Jefferson's departure from France, in 1789, William Short, his protégé and confidential secretary, left in Paris as chargé d'affaires, was pressed into service, and it is not unusual to find among the diplomatic papers that were dispatched across the sea detailed instructions "de faire cuire un poulet en cassette," or some other delicacy. Short even made a special trip to Naples to secure a "maccaroni mould" for Jefferson, in order that his patron might indulge in this favorite food. He writes: "It is of a smaller diameter than that used at the manufactories of maccaroni, but of the same diameter with others that have been sent to gentlemen in other countries. I went to see them made. I observed that the maccaroni most esteemed at Naples was smaller than that generally seen at Paris. This is the part of Italy most famous for the excellence of the article." Short was unaware that among the macaroni-cognoscenti this was known as spaghetti.

Lemaire, Jefferson's faithful maître d'hôtel during his presidency, contributed a disquisition on the use of wines in cooking: "Facon Demployer differents sorte de vin a Lusage de la cuisine francaise," probably our earliest written record, in America, of this refinement in the art of cooking. The author's orthographical accomplishments were scarcely greater in French than in English.

Boef a la mode	½ peinte de vin blanc
Veau a l'estaufade	½ idem de blanc
Dindon a la daube	½ idem de blanc
Matelot de paicon	½ idem de rouge
Une fricassee de lupin	½ idem de rouge
Un Gâteau au ri	une peinte de sherry, pour la sauce mariné
Les Beg'nais de pomme	½ Goblet d'au vie
Les Beg'nais de pain	½ peinte de madeira
Poutain a l'anglaise	1 peinte pour la sauce

From Petit, who entered his service in Paris as valet de chambre and was subsequently promoted to the rank of maître d'hôtel "in consequence of embezzlements and depredations committed by M. Marc, the late controller of Finances in his Department," Jefferson secured a recipe for making coffee which he ever after used. The terse annotation concluding the "rule" is but one of the many evidences of the meticulous care with which the President watched every detail of his household.

On one measure of the coffee ground into meal pour three measures of boiling water, boil it, on hot ashes mixed w. coal, till the meal disappears from the top, when it will be precipitated. Pour it three times through a flannel strainer, it will yield 2⅓ measures of clear coffee. An ounce of coffee meal makes 1½ cups of clear coffee in this way. The flannel must be rinced out in hot or cold water for every making.

Tea was likewise subject to his careful scrutiny and scientific observation, as well as sugar. He notes in his account book:

Feb. 8.

Tea out. The pound has lasted exactly 7 weeks, used 6 times a week. This is ⁸⁄₂₁ or .4 of an oz. a time, for a single person. A pound of tea making 126 cups costs 2 D. 126 cups or ounces of coffee = 8 lb. cost 1.6. Campbell, 1 lb. Imperial tea 2.

Feb. 18.

on trial it takes 11 dwt Troy of double refd maple sugar to a dish of coffee or 1 lb. avoirdupoise to 26.5 dishes, so that at 20 cents per lb. it is 8 mills per dish. An ounce of coffee at 20 cents per lb. is 12.5 mills so that sugar & coffee for a dish is worth two cents.

During the years he was president Jefferson found time to keep a careful table of the earliest and latest appearance of each vegetable on the Washington market. No less than thirty-seven kinds are listed. It is noteworthy that such delicacies as mushrooms, broccoli, and endive, which have become a commonplace on the American market only in the last decade, were no strangers to the presidential table in 1800. Broccoli is listed as being in season from April seventh to twentieth, mushrooms from the eleventh of August to the nineteenth of October—an odd season from our point of view, and endive from September twenty-seventh to February twenty-ninth.

Not only was such a minute account kept of the seasonable vegetables in market, but, in his "Garden Book,"

Jefferson likewise noted the time each vegetable grown at Monticello was sown, its name and "pedigree," for he often imported seeds or got them from neighbors or friends, along with the time it came to table. Thus, in 1774, after minute and elaborate annotations as to the planting of his garden, and whether the seeds were from Italy, from England, from Tuckahoe, from Dr. Brown or Colonel Bland, to mention only a few of his sources, he observes:

May	14	Cherries ripe.
	16	First dish of peas from earliest patch.
	26	A second patch of peas come to table.
June	4	Windsor beans come to table.
	5	A third and fourth patch of peas come to table.
	13	A fifth patch of peas come in.
July	13	Last dish of peas.
	18	Last lettuce from Gehee's.
	23	Cucumbers from our garden.
	31	Watermelons from our patch.
Aug.	3	Indian corn comes to table.
		Black-eyed peas come to table.
Nov.	16	The first frost sufficient to kill anything.

To a practical knowledge of the art of cookery Jefferson added a theoretical one. In his library, catalogued under the "Technical Arts" we find this imposing list of "cook books":

The London Country Brewer, 8vo; Cimbrini's Theory and Practice of Brewing, 8vo; Knight on the Apple and Pear, Cider and Perry, 12mo; Apicii Coelius de opsoniis et Condimentis, sive Arte Coquinaria, 12mo. apud Waistburgios, Amerdam MDCCIX; Avis au peuple sur leur premier besoin (le pain) par l'Abbé Baudan, 12mo. Amsterdam MDCCLXXIV; Avis sur la manière de faire le pain, par Parmentier, 12mo; Le Parfait Boulanger, par Parmentier, Paris MDCCLXXVIII, 8vo; Parmentier sur les Pommes de Terre (learned treatise) Paris, MDCCLXXXI, 12mo; Eale's cookery, 12mo; Dictionaire Domestique, 30 12mo. Paris MDCCLXIV; Kraft's American Distiller, 8vo; Tracts on Potash & Maple Sugar, Williamos, Hopkins remarks on Maple Sugar, 8vo; Resultats de la Fabrication des Sirops et des Conserves de Raisins, par Parmentier, 8vo. Paris 1812.

During his travels in Europe Jefferson made a point of sampling the foods and fruits of the locality through which he was passing. Thus in Holland he first tasted waffles and promptly bought a waffle iron for 1.3 florins. In Amsterdam it was Hyson's tea that pleased him and he carried along half a pound for 2 florins 13. At Nancy he notes paying "1 franc 4 for chocolate," and in his tour of southern France he made a comparative gustatory study of oranges in the various towns he visited. Ortolans also came under his notice; he paid 6 francs for a dozen of them at Nice. At Rozzano he took elaborate notes on the making of butter and Parmesan cheese and observed, on sampling a frozen delicacy, that "snow gives the most delicate flavor to creams, but ice is the most powerful congealer and lasts longer." On his return to the United States he found the luxuries to which he had become accustomed sadly wanting, and Petit, who followed him, was instructed to "bring a stock of macaroni, Parmesan cheese, figs of Marseilles, Brugnoles, raisins, almonds, mustard, vinaigre d'Estragon, other good vinegar, oil and anchovies."

Jefferson was the first to introduce vanilla to this country as well as macaroni. In 1791, when Secretary of State, he wrote from Philadelphia to William Short, the American chargé at Paris:

> Petit informs me that he has been all over the town in quest of vanilla, & it is unknown here. I must pray you to

send me a packet of 50 pods (batons) which may come very well in the middle of a packet of newspapers. It costs about 24 s a baton when sold by the single baton. Petit says there is a great imposition in selling those which are bad; that Piebot generally sells good, but that still it will be safe to have them bought by some one used to them.

It was as a connoisseur of wines, however, that Jefferson outshone all his contemporaries. He regarded wine, to use his own words, "as a necessity of life." "I rejoice as a moralist," he wrote toward the end of his life, "at the prospect of a reduction of the duties on wine, by our national legislature. It is an error to view a tax on that liquor as merely a tax on the rich. It is a prohibition of its use to the middling class of our citizens, and a condemnation of them to the poison of whiskey, which is desolating their houses. No nation is drunken where wine is cheap; and none sober, where the dearness of wine substitutes ardent spirits as the common beverage. It is, in truth, the only antidote to the bane of whiskey. Fix but the duty at the rate of other merchandise, and we can drink wine here as cheap as we do grog; and who will not prefer it? Its extended use will carry health and comfort to a much enlarged circle. Every one in easy circumstances (as the bulk of our citizens are) will prefer it to the poison to which they are now driven by their government. And the treasury itself will find that a penny apiece from a dozen, is more than a groat from a single one. This reformation, however, will require time."

During his travels through France and Germany in 1788, Jefferson made an extensive study of the vintage and the cultivation of grapes, not only for the sake of importing the wines, but also to introduce the culture to Virginia, something he had attempted even before the Revolution. From his faithful account book we observe that this was always in his thoughts. Thus he mentions, on April 10, 1788, at Hocheim, buying one hundred vines for 2f.15, and the same day, at Rudesheim, fifty vines for the same price. These were destined, of course, for America. The travel notes he made at this time are a learned treatise on viniculture. Nothing is omitted, from the imposing list beginning with Le Comte de Sichen, Le Comte d'Oschenstein, L'Electeur de Mayence, Le Comte de Meternisch, whose estates were said to yield the best crops and which produced the famous Schloss Johannisberger, to the important information that "the vignerons of Rudesheim dung their vines about once in five years, putting a one-horse tumbrel load of dung on every twelve feet square."

It was thus no accident that Jefferson's friends should come to rely upon his taste and knowledge. In 1790 we find him ordering sixty-five dozen bottles of wine for the President, George Washington, and as late as 1818 all but half a dozen lines of the letter of congratulation he wrote the new President, James Monroe, were devoted to a disquisition on the best wines of the time for official entertaining.

During his own administration the President's house was famous alike for its cuisine and its cellar. The amount consumed was appalling, according to our present standards. As usual Jefferson kept careful account and made most detailed estimates. He noted, on March 20, 1804, "there remain on hand 40 bottles of the 247 of champagne received from Fulwer Skipwith December 1. The consumption, then has been 207 bottles, which on 651 persons dined is a bottle to $3\frac{1}{7}$ persons. Hence the annual stock necessary may be calculated at 415 bottles a year, or say 500."

The five hundred bottles of champagne were a mere beginning. From a list of "wine provided at Washington," preserved among the Jefferson papers, we learn that in

1801 the President bought "five pipes of Brazil Madeira, a pipe of Pedo Ximenes Mountain (126 gallons, 424 bottles of it sent to Monticello); a quarter cask of Tent; a keg of Pacharetté doux; 400 bottles of claret; 540 bottles of Sauterne." The record for the following years is no less magnificent.

Hospitality at the President's house during Jefferson's administration took on something of the free and easy character of a bachelor's establishment, and it was always on a lavish scale. While in France Jefferson had formed "the habit of mitigating business with dinner," to which he always afterwards adhered. He entertained informally at dinner every day at four o'clock. The company usually numbered fourteen and was, as a contemporary remarked, "selected in reference to their tastes, habits and suitability in all respects, which attempt had a wonderful effect in making his parties more agreeable than dinner parties usually are." A French cook reproduced many of the delicacies Jefferson had learned in France, and added a number of his own. "Never before," one of his guests remarked, "had such dinners been given in the President's house, nor such a variety of the finest and most costly wines. In his entertainments republican simplicity was united with epicurean delicacy; while the absence of splendor, ornament and profusion was more than compensated by the neatness, order, and elegant sufficiency that pervaded the whole establishment. . . ."

It was left to a New England clergyman to complain that fried eggs and fried beef were served at the same dinner with turkey, ducks, and rounds of beef, but he was consoled by tasting for the first time "the new foreign dish, macaroni," by sampling ices and "a new kind of pudding, very porous and light, inside white as milk, and covered with cream sauce." This may well have been the very "Blanc Manger" for which Jefferson acquired the following recipe in Paris:

4 oz sweet almonds, with 5 or 6 bitter almonds

pour boiling water on them to take off the skin

put them in a mortar and beat them with a little cream

take them out of the mortar and liquify (delayer) them
   with cream little by little (peu à peu) stirring them

4 oz of sugar to be put in

have ready some isinglass (colle de poisson) say 1 oz dissolved in boiling water and pour it into the preceding
   mixture, stirring them well together

Strain it thro' a napkin, put it into a mould, and it is done.

In Jefferson's day, as now, the executive mansion boasted of two dining rooms, a large one on the northwest corner and a smaller one on the south front. It was here that Jefferson gathered his friends about him. The room was elaborately furnished, as an inventory in Jefferson's own hand assures us. There was an "elegant side board with pedestals and urn knife cases, a large Mahogany Dining Table in six pieces, a Small dining Table in three parts, a large Mahogany Square Table, two Glass Cases to contain the Silver and plated ware, an Oval breakfast Table, and fifteen chairs, black and gold." Chintz curtains, then the height of fashion, hung at the windows, and the walls were decorated with "two elegant Girandoles and two looking Glasses." The floor was covered by a canvas cloth, painted green. In Jefferson's own words, this was "laid down on the floor of the dining room when the table is set and taken up when the table is removed, merely to secure a very handsome floor from grease and the scouring which that necessitates."

Jefferson had a particular aversion to the presence of servants while he was at table, "believing," as one writer says, "that much of the domestic and even public discord was produced by the mutilated and misconstructed repetition of free conversation at dinner tables, by these mute but not inattentive listeners." To avoid this he had brought back from France the idea of the "dumb waiter," a sort of stand with shelves, containing everything for the dinner from beginning to end. This was placed between the guests and enabled them to serve themselves. There were five of these in the private dining room of the executive mansion. Jefferson went even farther than this, as we learn from one of his guests. "There was in his dining room an invention for introducing and removing the dinner without the opening and shutting of doors. A set of circular shelves were so contrived in the wall, that on touching a spring they turned into the room loaded with the dishes placed on them by the servants without the wall, and by the same process the removed dishes were conveyed out of the room."

Despite his distinguished position Jefferson was beset with many of the vexations familiar to every householder. It was, apparently, no more simple a matter to obtain a good cook in his day than it is in ours. Among his papers is a curious document in Jefferson's own hand, executed in Philadelphia not long before he resigned as Secretary of State, in which he agrees to set free one James Hemings, negro, provided the latter will return with him to Monticello and properly train a new cook. The agreement reads:

> Having been at great expence in having James Hemings taught the art of cookery, desiring to befriend him, and to require from him as little in return as possible, I do hereby promise & declare, that if the said James shall go with me to Monticello in the course of the ensuing winter, when I go to reside there myself, and shall there continue until he shall have taught such person as I shall place under him for that purpose to be a good cook this previous condition being performed, he shall be thereupon made free, and I will thereupon execute all proper instruments to make him free. Given under my hand and seal in the county of Philadelphia and the state of Penn-

sylvania this 15th day of September one thousand seven
hundred and ninety three

Witness

Adrien Petit   TH. JEFFERSON

With his election to the Presidency Jefferson's domestic
troubles began in earnest. Not only was he confronted
with an unfinished and half furnished executive mansion,
which he immediately set about furnishing in the latest
manner, but he was obliged to build up another household staff in addition to the one at Monticello. He did not
adopt what might have been the easiest, certainly, the
cheapest way, and bring some of his numerous slaves to
the White House, but employed free whites whom he
paid from his salary. Shortly before his inauguration we
find him writing "Citizen" La Tombe, one of his French
correspondents in Philadelphia:

> . . . I find great difficulty in composing my house-
> hold. . . . You know the importance of a good maître
> d'hôtel in a large house and the impossibility of finding
> one among the natives of our country. I have imagined
> that such a person might be found, perhaps, among the
> French of Philadelphia, that no one would be more likely
> to know it than yourself, and that no one would be a
> better judge of his qualifications. Honesty and skill in
> making the dessert are indispensable qualifications, that
> he should be good humoured and of a steady, discreet
> disposition is also important. If there be such a one within

the compass of your knowledge will you have the goodness to engage him to come to me immediately? . . . I
have a good cook, but it is *pour l'office*, & to take charge of
the family that I am distressed.

That Jefferson's difficulties were not at an end, and that
the "good cook" apparently gave notice upon survey-
ing the lack of facilities in the half-finished White House
we may gather from the appeal made to the Chevalier
d'Yrugo, the Spanish Minister to the United States: "I
have understood that twenty dollars a month is what is
given to the best French cook," Jefferson writes, "however, the Chevalier d'Yrugo having been so kind as to un-
dertake to get the one which he deemed the best in Philadelphia, I authorized him to go as high as twenty-eight
dollars."

Thanks to the efforts of Citizen La Tombe and the
Spanish Minister, a staff of eleven servants was presently
organized, Joseph Rapin was engaged as maître d'hôtel,
at $62.27 per month, although he was later succeeded by
Etienne Lemaire, who demanded only twenty dollars;
one Julien became chef, at twenty-five dollars, and Noël,
the garçon de cuisine, received eight. Edy and Fanny, two
slaves from Monticello, were taken to the White House to
learn French cooking, and when Jefferson finally retired
to Monticello they became his cooks there. During his
Washington days it was no uncommon sight early in the
morning to see the President drive with his maître d'hôtel
to the market in Georgetown and take a hand in selecting
the provisions for the day.

The cost of Jefferson's table was very great, even for
that time, and in spite of his careful calculations. During
the first year of his presidency, his income failed to meet
the expenditures. In an analysis he made on March 4,
1802, we find that he had spent $4,504.84 for provisions,
$2,003.71 for groceries, $2,797.28 for wines, to say noth-

ing of $2,675.84 for his servants. Lemaire frequently spent fifty dollars upon a single day's marketing. In addition to the supplies purchased in Alexandria, Georgetown, and Richmond, things were constantly being sent from Monticello. Jefferson himself always ordered the provisions that were purchased on a large scale for the President's house, as well as for Monticello. Entertaining never ceased, even when he took his holiday. It is interesting to note what was required on the plantation for Jefferson's annual spring visit:

> two pipes Marsalla; two casks Bucellas and Termo; five casks 50 doz. porter; 40 beef's tongues; 100 ham of Col. Mason, 4 kegs tomp and sounds, 40 lb. crackers; 5 bottles anchovies, 3 do pickles, 10 lb. almonds in a bag; 2 oz. cinnamon, 2 oz. nutmeg; 1 lb. allspice, 1 lb. pepper; 6 bottles mustard; 6 lb. chocolate, 6 lb. sugar; 20½ good cheese, 11¾ lb. ordinary; 40 lb. coffee; 10 lb. rice, 10 lb. pearl barley; 25 lb. raisins; 1 box sausages.

It is small wonder that such lavish entertaining should have made great inroads upon Jefferson's fortune. There were few men in America at the time who could have borne the burden, least of all a Virginia planter whose land was decreasing in value with every year. With his frugal New England outlook John Adams once remarked: "I dined a large company once or twice a week. Jefferson dined a dozen every day. I held levees once a week. Jefferson's whole eight years was a levee." John Adams had failed to understand the hospitality of the South, a hospitality by which Jefferson was quite literally eaten out of house and home.

When Jefferson ended his second term as President in 1808, and retired to Monticello, he was, for the first time since his earliest youth, able to lead the life he had always wished—that of a Virginia country gentleman. He was, to be sure, sixty-five years of age, but in his case it may very truly be said that he was sixty-five years young. He was to have eighteen years still before him, and he enjoyed them as he enjoyed perhaps, no other period of his life. His daughter, Martha Jefferson Randolph, presided over his household in the place of the wife he had lost so long ago, and his numerous grandchildren formed, in truth, a second family. He was as solicitous about their training and education as he had been about that of his own daughters. He had written to his own Polly, while Secretary of State, "I am much pleased with the account you give me of your occupations, and the making of the pudding is as good an article of them as any. When I come to Virginia I shall insist on eating a pudding of your own making, as well as on trying other specimens of your skill." He found time, as President, to send similar communications to each little granddaughter as she reached the age when the domestic virtues were to be cultivated. He suggested the books they read and the subjects they study; he was constantly sending them clippings of verse or other things of interest from the magazines and papers that passed through his hands, for them to paste in the scrapbooks he taught them to keep, and on resuming family life again at Monticello he talked with them about their books and the progress of their studies.

The Duke de la Rochefoucauld-Liancourt, whom Jefferson knew in France and who was a visitor at Monticello, has left an amiable picture of Jefferson as the master of Monticello: "In private life Mr. Jefferson displays a mild, easy, and obliging temper, though he is somewhat cold and reserved. His conversation is of the most agreeable kind, and he possesses a stock of information not inferior to that of any other man. In Europe he would hold a distinguished rank among men of letters, and as such he has already appeared there. At present he is employed with activity and perseverance in the management of his farms and buildings; and he orders, directs, and pursues in the minutest details every branch of business relative to them. I found him in the midst of the harvest, from which the scorching heat of the sun does not prevent his attendance. His negroes are nourished, clothed, and treated as well as white servants could be. As he can not expect any assistance from the two small neighboring towns, every article is made on his farm: his negroes are cabinet makers, carpenters, masons, bricklayers, smiths, etc. The children he employs in a nail factory, which yields already a considerable profit. The young and old negresses spin for the clothing of the rest. He animates them by rewards and distinctions; in fine, his superior mind directs the management of his domestic concerns with the same abilities, activity, and regularity which he evinced in the conduct of public affairs, and which he is calculated to display in every situation of life."

The busy day at Monticello began with a nine o'clock breakfast at which all the family and guests assembled. Jefferson had been up since dawn, busy with his correspondence. After breakfast, which was of the sturdy, Virginia variety—Daniel Webster mentions having hot breads and cold meats—with bacon and eggs and fried apples, and with the batter-cake express running at full speed between the kitchen and dining room, Jefferson visited his flower beds and garden, always in the company of several of his grandchildren. He then retired to his library, where he worked until one o'clock. At this hour his horse was brought and he rode about the plantation for an hour or two. Dinner was served at half-past three o'clock "in half Virginian, half French style, in good taste and abundance," Webster remarks. At six o'clock coffee and tea were brought to the drawing room. "He sat some time at table," one of his granddaughters writes, "and after dinner returned for a while to his room, from which he emerged before sunset, to walk on the terrace or the lawn, to see his grandchildren run races, or to converse with his family and friends. The evenings, after candle-light, he passed with us, till about ten o'clock. He had his own chair and his own candle, a little apart from the rest, where he sat reading, if there were no guests to require his attention, but often laying his book on his little round table or his knee, while he talked with my mother." Jefferson's reading chair and table were by the fireplace in the dining room, where the family seems to have spent a good deal of time, especially in winter. The dining room, just to the right of the sunny drawing room, where the mornings were passed when guests were present, opens on to a semioctagonal tea room, in which dinner was frequently served.

When Jefferson retired to Monticello his daughter is said to have asked him on what scale he wished to live, and he is supposed to have answered: "I will live like a plain country gentleman." It did not take him long to discover that this was to be impossible. The American public of the early nineteenth century took quite as much interest in its ex-presidents as the public of today, even more so in the case of the distinguished author of the Declaration of Independence. The visitors to Monticello were legion; they assumed something of the proportions of a bonus army. As one of Jefferson's granddaughters said of them: "They came of all nations, at all times, and paid longer or shorter visits. I have known a New England judge to bring a letter of introduction to my grandfather, and stay three weeks. The learned Abbé Correa, always a welcome guest, passed some weeks of each year with us during the whole time of his stay in the country. We had persons from abroad, from all States of the Union, from every part of the State—men, women, and children. In short, almost every day, for at least eight months of the year, brought its contingent of guests. People of wealth, fashion, men in office, professional men, military and civil, lawyers, doctors, Protestant clergymen, Catholic priests, members of Congress, foreign ministers, missionaries, Indian agents, tourists, travellers, artists, strangers, friends. Some came from affection and respect, some from curiosity, some to give or receive advice or instruction, some from idleness, some because others set the example, and very varied, amusing, and agreeable was the society afforded by this influx of guests. I have listened to very remarkable conversations carried on round the table, the fireside, or in the summer drawing-room. . . .

"There were few eminent men of our country, except perhaps, some political adversaries, who did not visit him in his retirement, to say nothing of distinguished foreigners. Life at Monticello was on an easy and informal footing. Mr. Jefferson always made his appearance at an early breakfast, but his mornings were most commonly devoted to his own occupations, and it was at dinner, after dinner, and in the evening, that he gave himself up to the society of his family and his guests. Visitors were left free to employ themselves as they liked during the morning hours—to walk, read, or seek companionship with the ladies of the family and each other. M. Correa passed his time in the fields and the woods; some gentlemen preferred the library; others the drawing-room; others the quiet of their own chambers; or they strolled down the mountain side and under the shade of the trees. The ladies in like manner consulted their ease and inclinations, and whiled away the time as best they might."

As there were no near-by taverns, and furthermore, as it was the custom of the country to ask a visitor to have a meal, if not to spend the night, Jefferson was soon in a position to feel about Monticello much as Washington once expressed himself about Mount Vernon—that his home was a well-resorted inn. Within two years of Jefferson's retirement it was found necessary to employ thirty-seven house servants at Monticello, and the whole estate was unable to furnish enough food for the guests, their servants and horses. It is said that Mrs. Randolph, upon whose capable shoulders the burden of this vast amount of entertaining rested, once observed that fifty unexpected guests was the largest number she had ever been called upon to house overnight. "I have never seen her at all disturbed by any amount of care or trouble," the overseer of Monticello was able to remark after knowing her and serving her for more than twenty years.

The tradition of fine cooking was carried on at Monticello, as it had been at the White House, and inherited by Jefferson's grandchildren. Each of the six granddaughters, as thoroughly schooled in the domestic arts as in French, Latin, or music, carefully copied, in the delicate handwriting they had learned from their mother, the favorite "rules" and "receipts" of the household, whether from Lemaire, the President's steward, from Julien, the chef, Petit, the old stand-by, Annette, or some friend. Sometimes they were taken from a receipt book much used in the family. The pages of these hand-written cook books are neatly bound together in little volumes, if they may so be called, with a bit of slender but carefully tied cord. There is a "volume" on soups, one on "Made Dishes," a third on "Creams etc." and a fourth on puddings. Greatly prized, these Monticello cook books were carried by the brides of the family to their new homes, as one of their greatest treasures.

To the present-day cook some of the receipts may seem incredibly archaic and amusing, as, for example, the one for chocolate or coffee cream. This was nothing more than elaborate junket, but instead of reaching casually for a junket tablet and preparing the dessert in less than five minutes, the skill of two persons was involved and much preparation in advance. The directions read:

> Put on your milk, 1 quart to 2 squares of chocolate; boil it away one quarter. Take it off, let it cool and sweeten it.

Lay a napkin in a bowl, put three gizzards in the napkin and pass the cream through it four times, as quick as possible, one person rubbing the gizzards with a spoon while another pours. Put it in cups and set the cups in cold water half way up their sides. Set the water on fire, cover it, and put fire on the top. As soon as the water boils, take the cups out and set them to cool.

The gizzards used for this purpose are only the inside skins, taken off as soon as the chicken is killed, washed, dried, and kept in paper bags in a dry place. The effect is the same with rennet.

The book of Monticello recipes here reproduced is the one made by Virginia Randolph, Martha Jefferson Randolph's fifth daughter, who was born in 1801 and who, in 1821, married Nicholas P. Trist, later our envoy to Mexico. On her death it passed to her only daughter, Martha Jefferson Trist, and subsequently to the latter's daughter, Fanny M. Burke of Alexandria. Miss Burke presented the book to the Thomas Jefferson Memorial Foundation, shortly before her death, and joined with the Foundation in giving the editor permission to prepare it for publication. As here given the recipes are adapted for modern use—the dozen eggs and pound of butter common to an earlier era being not only appalling in quantity, but terrifying in price to the householder of the present day. They have been proportioned to our current practice of a formula for serving six persons, and the directions for cooking, or baking, or boiling, as the case may be, have been adapted and tested to suit an electric or gas stove, rather than meet exigencies of cooking over a crane or submitting one's chef d'œuvre to the questionable mercies of a hot shovel or poker. Gelatine has been substituted for calves' hoofs, junket for chicken gizzard, and our useful American food chopper for mortar and pestle.

[1]The recipe for *sauce hachée* is not given by Jefferson, but in Prosper Montagné's great cook book we find it is made as follows: Cook one tablespoon of finely chopped onion in some butter very slowly, without letting it brown. When tender add one-half tablespoon of chopped shallot. Cook for a moment or two, then moisten with one-third of a cup of vinegar and the same amount of white wine. Add two-thirds cup of Spanish sauce and one-half cup of tomato sauce. Boil gently for five minutes. Just before serving add a tablespoon of duxelles preparation, a tablespoon of lean ham cut in tiny cubes and a teaspoon of capers.

[2]Soup of small roots is attributed to Carême, the great French cook. It is made as follows: Chop six carrots, six turnips, four onions, ten leeks and two celery roots. Brown slowly in butter, add 1 quart of boiling water, salt and pepper to taste and cook until vegetables are tender. Press through a very fine sieve, add 1 cup cream. Bring to boiling point and pour into soup tureen containing small croutons.

[3]This sauce, says Montagné, is a very complicated one, scarcely feasible today. Broth made of veal, fowl, ham and various vegetables, is the foundation, with a great deal of butter and chopped mushrooms.

Thomas Jefferson's Paris Recipes

During the first year and a half of his residence in Paris
Jefferson did not keep house in the accepted sense of the
word. He had, to be sure, an establishment with four
French servants besides his faithful slave, James Has-
tings, whom he had brought with him from America.
His meals, however, were either sent in to him, or he
went out for them. In the minute account of his expenses
which he kept, we find that each week he paid the *traiteur*, or innkeeper, from seventy to two hundred and forty
francs. On December 16, 1785, after he had moved into
the *hôtel* of the Count de Langeac, which was to be his
permanent home, he engaged a cook. She seems to have
started on her duties on the first of January, 1786, for
Jefferson notes giving her the usual French New Year's
gift on that day, along with similar ones to the other servants. Furthermore, for the first time since he came to

Paris, his accounts show an item for kitchen expenses—
432 francs 16 sous for the period from January first to
eighth. The payments to the *traiteur* cease.

Keeping house in the most fashionable capital in the
world was a very different thing from running a plantation. Setting an elegant table with due regard for hal-
lowed sauces and proper combinations of food, was an art
to be mastered. Jefferson set about this with his usual
thoroughness. As a first step, in December, 1784, he sent
James to a *traiteur* to be taught the art of cookery. He likewise applied his own talents to the problem and it is
likely that at this time he wrote the notes that here follow.
They are a list of suitable methods of cooking various
viands and, often, of the proper sauces to accompany
them. The manuscript, written in French, with a few
English interlineations, was found in the Coolidge Col-
lection of the Massachusetts Historical Society, and is
here presented in translation by their kind permission:

Beef	Glazed rump of beef with *sauce hachée.*[1]
	Soup of small roots.[2]
	ditto, purée of peas or beans.
	ditto, of noodles or Italian paste (maca-roni).
Mutton	Mutton cutlet, crumbed and broiled.
	ditto, with sweet herbs, onion, etc., cut fine.
	ditto, with small roots in various ways.
	Shoulder of mutton, larded and roasted.
Veal	Noisette of veal, larded and broiled.
	Cutlets in paper.
	ditto, crumbed and broiled.
	ditto, stewed, with garnish of small car-rots and onions.

Lamb	Roast hindquarter; the same with the forequarter.

Entrées of veal, a ragout with small roots (such as carrots, celery roots, turnips and beets cut in small shapes), or with sorrel.
Slices of ragout, larded and glazed.

Sauces	Jellied, sauce tournée,[3] glazed, beef gravy, broth.

[Veal]	Veal olives. Slice of veal crumbed and fried in butter (for turkey galantine). Slices of veal between bacon with force-meat rolled in. Veal cutlet, Breast of veal, stuffed. Rump, stuffed and larded, calves feet marinated and fried. Calves head, boiled with a sharp, vinegar sauce. Calves liver, larded and stuffed, with a sauce.

Beef	Larded and braised. Ditto, broiled with *sauce hachée*. Ditto, with gravy.

Fowl	Capon with clear gravy; pullet boned and stuffed. Chicken, fricasseed, or with white or brown butter sauce. Ditto, marinated, crumbed and broiled. Stuffed with a variety of fillings and garnitures.

Pigeons	Stewed; broiled on a gridiron with their legs flattened and stretched out; pickled.

Duck	Fricasseed, cooked on the spit; with olives; boned and stuffed.

Turkey	Boiled, with a variety of garnishings.
	Ditto, stuffed, or braised.
	Ditto. A galantine of the same, jellied.
	Ditto. Filets of breast, larded and jellied.
	Ditto. The wings, crumbed, broiled or baked, with mustard sauce.
Game	Pheasants, larded and roasted.
	Partridges, ditto.
	Ditto, stewed with wine, onions and other small vegetables.
	Ditto, fricasseed, as are chickens.
	Ditto, crumbed and broiled.
Rabbit	Rabbit stew with bacon and small onions, claret or white wine. Red wine is the best.
	Ditto, boned and stuffed.
	Ditto, larded and glazed.
	Ditto, broiled with a shallot sauce.
	Ditto. Larded filets, glazed, on purée of sorrel.
Fish	Stew (called matelote) of eel, catfish, pike or other fish, with red wine, small onions and mushrooms.
	Ditto, with sweet herbs.
	Ditto, fried or baked.
	Ditto, boiled, with caper sauce.
Pastry	Vol-au-vent (a case of puff paste with raised border) with various fillings of meat or other things. Small patty shells with the same fillings.
	Small patty shells with gravy.
	Tart with a meat or vegetable filling, with eggs or other things.

Fresh pork	Cutlets with sauce Robert (one of the oldest French sauces).
	Ditto, the head made into headcheese, or a galantine.
	Ditto. The feet, boiled in a light brine, crumbed and broiled.
	Ditto. Black pudding and sausage.
Roast veal	The loin is the best part to roast.
	The rump, slashed, with stuffing in the slashes, roasted with clear gravy. The breast the same way.
Roast mutton	And various meats, lamb, veal, pork.

Entrées

Roast fowl	Larded turkey, chickens, capons, guineas, pigeons, ducks, geese, Muscovy ducks or Barbary Coast ducks.
Game	Larded pheasants, partridges, rabbits, woodcocks, snipe, plovers.
Venison	Larded and marinated in diluted vinegar with basil, onions, parsley, carrots and a little garlic chopped fine. Serve with sauce Piquante (a sauce made with vinegar, herbs and other sharp ingredients).
Vegetables	Cooked with meat or without.
	Spinach, garnished with croutons, if you wish, or with milk and a little sugar.
	Chicory with white sauce.
	String beans with sweet herbs.
	Ditto with white sauce.

Peas, with sugar, or with hearts of lettuce.

Celery, cooked in various ways.

Sorrel with eggs.

Turnips with butter sauce.

Cabbage, ditto.

Carrots, ditto.

Potatoes, fried; without their jackets, cut in small slices and served with various sauces.

Kidney beans, brown sauce with onions.

Cauliflower, ditto.

Artichokes, ditto.

Salsify, dipped in batter and fried, or with butter sauce.

Bacon omelet.

Pastries for Dessert

All sorts of tarts   Apples, cream, frangipane (a sort of custard made with milk, sugar, eggs, a thickening agent and pulverized almonds).

Small pastries of puff paste in various shapes, garnished with jelly, gooseberries or apples.

Dishes made with milk   Little pots of custard.

Rice pudding.

Small meringues with cream.

Custard glazed with a hot poker.

Custard with cream.

Potato soufflée.

Cream soufflée.

Omelet soufflée.

Creams of various sorts.

Blanc mange with almonds.
Wine jelly.

Fruits   Compote of apple, whole or in pieces.
Ditto, of pears.
Ditto, of cherries.
Ditto, of strawberries.
Ditto, of orange.

Little cakes   Sponge cakes in cases. One pound of
sugar, ½ pound of flour, 16 eggs.
Sponge cake in a form. ¾ pound flour for
1 pound sugar.

Almonds   Macaroons, pound for pound.
Ditto, burnt almonds, pound for pound.
Pancakes, ditto.

Fritter batter, 1 pound flour, ¾ pound butter, 2 eggs
(liquid omitted).

Ices of various kinds and meringues.

Ice Cream

Beat the yolks of 6 eggs until thick and lemon colored. Add, gradually, 1 cup of sugar and a pinch of salt. Bring to a boil 1 quart of cream and pour slowly on the egg mixture. Put in top of double boiler and when it thickens, remove and strain through a fine sieve into a bowl. When cool add 2 teaspoonfuls of vanilla. Freeze, as usual, with one part of salt to three parts of ice. Place in a mould, pack in ice and salt for several hours. For electric refrigerators, follow usual direction, but stir frequently.

Blanc Mange

Blanch and remove skins from ¼ pound almonds, along with 5 or 6 bitter almonds. Put through food chopper, using finest grinder. Add gradually, stirring constantly, 2 cups thin cream. Stir in 3 tablespoonfuls of sugar, and a few grains of salt. Soak 1 scant tablespoonful of gelatine in 2 tablespoonfuls cold water for five minutes. Dissolve in ¼ cup of boiling water. Add to almond mixture, stirring well together. Strain through a fine sieve, pour into moulds, "and it is done."

Biscuit de Savoye

Separate 6 eggs. Beat the yolks until lemon colored and light. Add 6 tablespoonfuls of sugar and the grated rind of one orange. Beat well; add 6 tablespoonfuls of sifted flour mixed with ⅛ teaspoonful of salt. Beat the egg whites until stiff and dry. Fold into the first mixture. Butter a cake mould and dust with sugar. Turn the mixture into this and set in a slow oven. Bake from thirty to forty minutes, or until cake shrinks from edge of pan.

Wine Jelly

Soak 2 tablespoonfuls of gelatine in ½ cup water for five minutes. Dissolve in 1 pint of milk that has been brought to a boil. Add ¾ cup of sugar and pinch of salt, let cool. Add 1 pint of Madeira wine and the juice of 3 lemons. Add more sugar if not sufficiently sweet. Strain through a double cheesecloth and pour into moulds.

Macaroons

Pour boiling water on 1 pound of almonds and remove the skin. Wash them in cold water. Wipe them well with a towel. Put them through a food chopper, using finest grinder. Turn into a wooden bowl and add gradually ¾ of a pound of powdered sugar, beating thoroughly all the while with a wooden spoon. Add, one by one, the whites of 3 eggs, beating constantly to a smooth paste. Drop from the tip of a spoon on white paper, in small balls about the size of a nut. Bake fifteen to twenty minutes in a slow oven.

Meringues

Beat the whites of 6 eggs to a stiff froth. Add, very gradually, 6 tablespoonfuls of sugar. With a tablespoon form them into rounds of desired size, on a piece of white paper. Put in a very slow oven. You may leave them there as long as you wish.

Noodles à la Macaroni

Beat 6 eggs until light, add 1 cup milk and ½ teaspoon salt. Add enough flour, about 4 cups, to make a thick dough. Roll, with a rolling pin, to ⅛-inch thickness. Cut into small pieces and roll these between the hands into long strips resembling macaroni. Cut them to a proper length. Drop into boiling, salted water and cook for fifteen minutes. Dress them as you would macaroni. They may also be served boiled in soup.

Brandied Peaches

Wipe off the peaches to remove the down. Prick them in four or five places with a fork. Drop them into boiling water for a moment, remove, and place immediately in cold water. Remove and let them drain. Make a syrup of sugar and a little water, using one pound of sugar to four pounds of peaches. Boil until, when you dip two fingers into it, they will stick together. Let cool. Add the peaches and let stand for twenty-four hours. Bring the syrup to a boil again and add 1 pint of brandy. Do not leave the syrup on the fire while you are doing this. You will burn your face if you do not take this precaution. Let the syrup cool again and add the peaches. The following day remove the peaches again, bring syrup to a boil and add as much brandy as you wish. Put in the peaches and let simmer until tender. Let them cool, then remove gently and put in jars. Strain the syrup over them through a cheesecloth.

The Monticello
Recipes

SOUPS

Observations on Soups

Always observe to lay your meat in the bottom of the pan with a lump of butter. Cut the herbs and vegetables very fine and lay over the meat. Cover it close and set over a slow fire. This will draw the virtue out of the herbs and roots and give the soup a different flavour from what it would have from putting the water in at first. When the gravy produced from the meat is almost dried up, fill your pan up with water. When your soup is done, take it up and when cool enough, skim off the grease quite clean. Put it on again to heat and then dish it up. When you make white soups, never put in the cream until you take it off the fire. Soup is better the second day in cool weather.   *Monticello*

Beef Soup

Take a shin of beef, or any offal piece, cut it up and fry it a light brown in 2 tablespoonfuls of butter, stirring it frequently to prevent its burning. Cover it entirely with water and let it come to a boil. Skim the foam that rises and boil slowly until the meat is tender and falls apart, adding more water, should it boil away too much. Take 3 onions, a small cabbage, 2 turnips, 2 parsnips, a stalk of celery and cut them in small, even pieces. Melt 3 tablespoonfuls of butter in a pan, add the vegetables and turn them over and over in the butter until well coated. Cover with some of the broth from the soup and cook slowly until thoroughly done. Season with salt and a very little pepper. Mix the whole together and serve.

The cabbage should not be put in until after the other vegetables are almost done, as it takes a shorter time to fry.

Monticello

Noodles to Thicken the Soup

Beat 3 eggs slightly, add ½ cup milk, 2 cups flour, ½ teaspoonful of salt. Mix together well. It should form a stiff dough. If necessary, add more flour. Roll out very thin, cut in small pieces, which roll again in long strips. They should be very thin. Then cut them again in strips about 2 inches long and ¼ of an inch wide and put them in the soup. If you mean to dress them as macaroni, drop them in boiling water, cover fifteen minutes and drain.

Soup à la Julienne

Take carrots, turnips and potatoes and cut them in strips about ¼ of an inch long and ½₂ of an inch wide. There should be ¾ cupful of each. Melt 2 tablespoonfuls of butter, add the vegetables and fry gently, stirring carefully, until they begin to shrivel. Then put them in the soup. When it boils, add ¼ cup of sorrel, and ½ cup of spinach, which should first have been scalded with boiling water to take the sharpness out, then drain and chop fine. Add to your Julienne also 3 stalks of celery and 2 beets cut up like turnips and carrots. Also ½ cup of green peas, when they are in season.

This soup should be made with beef broth, about 2½ quarts, or if water is used 3 spoonfuls of dried beans that have been soaked should be put in.

It should cook for two hours. Before serving cut 3 slices of bread in small cubes and brown in butter. Add to soup.

Annette

Mexican Bean Soup

To 3 quarts of water add 1 pint of black Mexican beans that have been thoroughly washed, and 2 pounds of shortribs of beef or a veal knuckle. Boil slowly for three to four hours, until the beans are soft. Pour through a colander and press the beans through. Simmer again for fifteen minutes, add salt and pepper to taste. Serve with small squares of bread that have been toasted and browned in butter. If intended for mock turtle soup, add a small glass of wine.

Receipt furnished by the grocer who sold the beans.

Pumpkin Soup

Take half a small pumpkin, peel, cut in small pieces and put on the stove with half a glass of water. When the pumpkin is tender, drain, and pass through a colander. Add 3 tablespoonfuls of butter; sugar, salt, and pepper to taste. Let it simmer for fifteen minutes. Add 4 cups boiling milk, stirring well while pouring it in. When well mixed, pour over croutons, made by cutting three slices of bread in small cubes and browning well in butter.

Annette

Potato Soup

Peel and cut 3 large potatoes in pieces. Cover with water and boil until tender. Put through a colander and add 3 cups of water. Bring to a boil, add salt to taste, 2 tablespoonfuls of butter, ¼ cup rice or a tablespoonful of tapioca. Cook for twenty-five minutes. Add 1 tablespoonful of sorrel, chopped fine. Beat the yolks of 3 eggs until light, add to the soup and serve. *Annette*

Where eggs are put into soup they should not be put into the pot on the fire, but after it has been removed. Tomatoes are a very good substitute for sorrel.

Pea Soup

Take 1 cup of green peas, drop into 2½ cups of boiling, salted water. Cook until tender. Drain, but keep the water for the soup. Pass peas through colander, add to water with ½ teaspoonful of sugar, ½ tablespoonful of chopped sorrel or parsley, or any other green vegetable, and thicken with 1 tablespoonful of flour mixed to a paste with 1 tablespoonful of butter. Add well beaten yolks of 2 eggs.

All other kinds of soup à la purée are made in the same manner, but if made of dry vegetables they should be put in cold water. *Annette*

Gumbo

One quart of okra, 1 quart of tomatoes, 1 pound of any kind of meat, but veal or chicken is best. Cut up the meat in small pieces and roll in flour. Put a large tablespoonful of butter into the soup pot and fry the meat until brown. Cut up 1 large onion and fry brown. Then add the okra that has been cut up, also the tomatoes peeled and cut in small pieces and fry brown. Let all cook together for fifteen minutes. Add 2 quarts of water; salt, pepper and herbs to taste. Cook four or five hours, stirring frequently. A pod of green pepper, cut up and added is a great improvement. *Mrs. G. W. Randolph*

Gumbo may be made with sassafras leaves dried and powdered, instead of okra, but the sassafras leaves must not be put in until the soup is done. Then add 2 tablespoonfuls of sassafras.

Okra Soup

Cut up 1 quart of okra, add 2 cups of water and bring to a boil. Half an hour later add 1 cup of lima beans, a pound of fresh meat cut up, or a fowl. An hour before serving add 5 tomatoes cut in pieces. When almost done put in a lump of butter as big as an egg, rolled in flour. Do not make it too thick. Put it on early and only let it simmer.

Mrs. Martha Randolph, Monticello

Okra Soup

Take the okra so young as to be crisp, about two or three inches long. They may be used as long as they are tender, which may be judged by their brittleness. If good, they snap; if they bend, they are too old. Slice 1 quart like cucumbers for eating, ½ inch thick. Add ⅓ the amount of tomatoes, more or less according to taste, a shin of beef, and 3 quarts of water. You may add 3 ears of young corn cut from the cob, and 2 cups of lima beans. The soup should boil for five hours. It will be reduced to one-half.

When done, the meat will be boiled to rags and quit the bone. The whole should be one homogeneous mass, in which none of the ingredients should be distinct. Its consistency should be just as thick as porridge; the color green, mixed with yellow or red from the tomatoes.

University of Virginia

Catfish Soup

To 2 quarts of water add 4 or 5 catfish, according to size, a slice of lean ham, 2 onions chopped fine, 3 sprigs of parsley, a bunch of sweet herbs, half a dozen pepper-corns, and a teaspoonful of salt. Boil until the fish go to pieces, strain, put on fire again with another fish that has been skinned and cut in pieces. Boil until fish is tender. Add ½ pint cream, 1 tablespoonful of flour, mixed to a paste with 2 tablespoonfuls of butter, and the yolks of 4 eggs. Serve with chopped parsley.

Oyster Soup

Stew 3 slices of bacon and 3 sprigs of parsley with a pint of water, and 1 quart of oysters which have been washed and drained. Stew for half an hour. Add 1 pint of cream, 3 tablespoonfuls of butter rolled in flour, and the yolk of 2 eggs. *Mrs. Martha Randolph*

Mutton Broth

Take 2 pounds of neck of mutton, wash it very well, let it soak in cold water one hour. Put it in a soup pot with 3 quarts of water and bring to a boil. Skim as often as the foam rises. Add ½ pint of barley. Let simmer for four hours. Two hours before serving add the vegetables, 6 car-rots, 3 stalks celery, 2 turnips, 1 onion, cut in fine pieces. Should the water boil away too much, add more, accord-ing to your own judgment. The salt and pepper you put in must be after your own taste.

When done, take out all the bones of the mutton, and the meat, which will, by this time, be done to rags.

Ellen Wayles Randolph Coolidge

Bean Soup

Put 2 cups of beans to soak in water to cover at night. The next morning put them into a pot with 1 teaspoonful of salt and 2 quarts of water. Bring to a boil and simmer slowly for an hour. Then add 6 carrots, 2 turnips, and 1 parsnip, scraped and cut into small, even pieces. Let the soup simmer for three or four hours, skimming when necessary. When the vegetables are soft press the whole through a colander and return to the pot. Scrape and cut 4 stalks of celery into small pieces and add to the soup. Let simmer until tender. If soup gets too thick add enough boiling water to make of proper consistency. Cut 4 slices of bread into small pieces, toast, and turn over and over in butter. Pour the soup over this and serve.

Gouverneur Morris the Elder

Pigeon Soup

Cut up 2 pigeons and put into 2 quarts of water, let simmer three hours. Strain, and put juice back into soup kettle with 4 sprigs of parsley and ½ cupful of spinach, finely chopped. Add 1 pint of cream in which ½ cupful of bread crumbs have been mixed. Cut up the pigeon meat in small pieces, season with salt and a little mace, and simmer in the soup for fifteen minutes.

Mrs. Horace Mann

Stock for Clear Soup

Cut up a knuckle of veal into small pieces. Place into a soup pot with 4 tablespoonfuls of butter and 3 teaspoonfuls of salt, ½ dozen peppercorns, 3 small onions sliced, 2 cloves, 6 carrots, 2 leeks, 1 turnip, 4 stalks of celery. To add more zest to the flavor add the smallest quantity of thyme, 1¼ teaspoonfuls winter savory in the same amount, and a bay leaf. Add 1 cup of water, set on stove and bring to a boil. When boiling stir for ten minutes, or until it forms a whitish, thick gravy at the bottom, or gets rather dry. Then add 5 pints of water. When it comes to a boil, let it simmer for ¾ of an hour. Stir it well, strain it through a cheesecloth and it will be found clear and ready for use. Take the fat off.   *Soyer*

White Soup

Put into a bowl ½ cup of flour, stir in slowly 1 cup of milk, ½ teaspoonful salt, ¼ teaspoonful pepper. Add gradually to the broth (in the quantity of the preceding recipe for stock). Boil gently for ten minutes, stirring constantly. Skim it. It may be poured over the veal, or have some more of the vegetables that were used in the stock, added. They should be cut small, fried, and simmered in the soup. Remove any fat. You may add a cup of rice, or macaroni, or vermicelli, previously boiled until tender. Fried or toasted bread, cut in dice, may be added.
          Soyer

A French Soup Maigre

Take a large lump of butter and a tablespoonful of flour. Brown them in the saucepan in which the soup is to be made. Chop until fine 6 carrots, 2 onions, 4 stalks of celery, 2 potatoes, and some sorrel. Mix them together, put them into the saucepan, add pepper and salt to taste, and pour on boiling water until generously covered. Let them stew for three or four hours. They can hardly simmer too long. A little thyme, parsley, cress and mint are a great improvement, added to the above ingredients.

Vegetable Porridge

Scrape and peel the following vegetables: 6 carrots, 6 turnips, 6 onions, 3 heads of celery, and 3 parsnips. Slice very thinly and put into a soup pot with 6 tablespoonfuls of butter. Add a bunch of parsley, a large sprig of thyme and fill the pot with water, about 4 quarts. Set on stove. Season to taste with salt and pepper. Boil very slowly for two hours. At the end of this time the vegetables will be cooked to a pulp. Press all through a colander with a wooden spoon. Return to pot and bring to a boil. Serve.

Pot au Feu

Take 3 pounds of beef, the short ribs are best, put in a soup kettle and cover well with cold water, about 3 quarts, and bring to a boil. Skim well. Add 1 tablespoonful of salt, 2 large carrots, 2 turnips, 1 parsnip, 3 large onions, each one with a clove stuck in it, a small piece of garlic, a bunch of leeks, and a small stalk of celery. Let it boil very slowly for five or six hours.   *Annette*

Gumbo

Put 2 tablespoonfuls of fat in a skillet and stir in gradually 1 tablespoonful of flour, 1 teaspoonful of chopped parsley and ½ an onion minced fine. When the flour is brown, add 1 fowl which has been disjointed, and let it brown. Add 4 pints of water and season with salt, black and red pepper. Let it boil gently for an hour and a half. Just before serving stir in, while stirring constantly, 2 or 3 tablespoonfuls of gumbo (sassafras leaves, dried and pounded) according to the amount of liquid in the pot. Do not let boil after the gumbo is put in. Turn into soup tureen and serve. *Mrs. Rosella Trist*

MEATS AND FOWL

Important Observations on Roasting, Boiling, and Frying

In roasting, the meat should be washed and wiped dry, sprinkled with salt and a little pepper, dredged with flour and put in a very hot oven. When the flour in the pan begins to brown, add a tablespoonful of shortening and baste the meat every ten minutes. Reduce the heat. Put ½ cup of water in pan and continue basting until meat is done and a nice, brown crust formed.

Beef and mutton must not be roasted as much as veal, lamb or pork. Veal may be served with a little melted butter on the platter, but all the others must be served without sauce. For those who must have gravy with these meats, let it be made in any way they like and served in a boat. A loin of lamb or a hindquarter of lamb should be served with the kidneys about the platter.

Whatever is to be boiled must be put in cold water with a little salt. When they are put in boiling water the outside is done too much before the inside is heated.

In choosing meat you must see that the fat is not yellow and that the lean parts are of a fine, close grain, a lively color, and will feel tender when pinched. Poultry should be well covered with white fat. If the bottom of the breastbone be gristly, it is young; but if a hard bone, it is an old one.

For broiling, sprinkle with a little salt and pepper and put broiler under a hot flame. When done, put on platter, pour over some melted butter and chopped parsley. This is for broiled veal, wild fowl, birds or poultry. Beefsteak and mutton chops require only a tablespoonful of hot water poured over.

To have viands served in perfection, the dishes should be made hot, either by setting them over hot water, or by putting some in them.

Rules to Be Observed in Made Dishes

If cream is to be used in them it must never be suffered to boil after it is put in, for fear of its turning.

Lemon juice or mushroom pickle should be put in just as you are about to serve them, otherwise they will curdle. The sauce should be smooth and of the thickness of cream.

Made dishes with a brown sauce should be a good thickness.

Care must be taken in seasoning that no one article should predominate and that your dish should be free from scum and fat. *Martha Jefferson Randolph*

A White Fricassee

Take 2 chickens, skin them, cut the joints asunder and lay them in warm water for fifteen minutes. Dry them and stew them slowly in half milk, half water, until tender. To 1 cup of milk and 1 cup of cream add 4 tablespoonfuls of butter. Simmer until thick. Cool, add a dash of mace, ½ nutmeg grated, ½ teaspoonful of salt, ½ cup of white wine and 1 cup of mushrooms. Stir well. Remove chickens from the liquor in which they were cooked, discard that, put chickens in the gravy and heat thoroughly. Serve.

Lamb, tripe and rabbits may be dressed the same way.

Mrs. Martha Randolph

To Stew Rabbits, Chickens or Ducks

Take a rabbit. Put a bunch of parsley and an onion in its belly. Parboil. Cut into pieces. Take the onion, parsley and liver and shred fine. Mix 3 tablespoonfuls of claret or Madeira with ½ of vinegar, and dissolve 2 anchovies in it. Put into the stewpan with a little of the liquor in which they were boiled. When tender thicken with 1 tablespoonful of butter rolled in flour. *Martha Jefferson Randolph*

Fricassee of Chicken

Cut 2 young chickens in pieces and put them in hot water. Let stand ten minutes. Remove the chickens, dry carefully and strain the water. Put 3 good tablespoonfuls of water in a saucepan and turn the chickens well in it. Add a tablespoonful of flour, stir well, and add the water in which the chickens were scalded. Simmer one-half hour. Add 6 small onions, a dozen mushrooms and a bunch of herbs. When the onions and mushrooms are done, the chickens ought to be done, also. Remove the chickens to a platter, add the yolks of 2 eggs to the gravy stirring vigorously. Pour over the chicken and serve. You can, if you like, beat in the juice of a lemon with the egg.

Annette

Chicken with Rice

Put your chicken into a casserole with 2 small onions which have cloves stuck into them, 3 carrots cut in fine slices, a bunch of parsley and some bits of veal, if you have any. Pour some stock on the chicken and vegetables until nearly covered. Cook gently for 2 hours. When the fowl is done pour the broth through a sieve and boil 6 tablespoonfuls of rice in it until tender. Put the chicken in the middle of a platter and surround with rice. *Annette*

Chicken à la Merengo

Cut up a fowl and brown in oil. Add 1 cupful of button mushrooms; salt, and pepper to taste, a very small piece of garlic, 1 teaspoonful of chopped parsley, a tablespoonful of chopped tomatoes or tomato sauce, a tablespoonful of meat jelly, and the juice of 1 lemon. Let simmer until the fowl is tender. If the sauce gets too dry, add a little water as it cooks.

*Capitolade of the Remains of Roast Fowl

Cut leftover pieces of fowl in small, even pieces. Put 2 tablespoonfuls of butter in a frying pan, add the fowl and stir well. Fry it with some chopped herbs and add 1 tablespoonful of flour, 1 cup chicken gravy, and 1 wine-glassful of white wine. Add salt to taste. Simmer for ten minutes. This dish is for breakfast. *Annette*

*A ragout of cold meat.

Pigeons in Compote

Take 4 good pigeons, draw them, wash well, dry and dust with salt and pepper. Make a brown gravy with stock and put your pigeons to cook in it for one and a half hours over a low fire. At the end of the first half-hour, add 2 sprigs of parsley, 1 cup of mushrooms, sliced, and 4 or 5 very small onions. The sauce should be thick. *Annette*

Pigeons à la Crapaudine

Split two pigeons through the stomach and flatten the backs with a bread knife. Broil for twenty-five minutes, taking care that they are evenly browned. Serve with tartar sauce. This dish is generally used for breakfast.

Annette

Civet of Hare

Melt 3 tablespoonfuls of butter and fry in it 12 small onions that have been carefully peeled. When a delicate brown, remove from the butter and add 1½ tablespoonfuls of flour. Stir well together. Add 1 hare which has been disjointed and stir in the butter mixture for five minutes. Add 1½ cups of white wine and 1½ cups of stock, salt and pepper to taste, and 3 sprigs of parsley. When the hare is nearly done, put back the onions and add 1 cup of button mushrooms. *Annette*

Croquettes of Roasted Veal

Put some roasted veal through a food chopper. There should be 2 cupfuls. Put 3 tablespoonfuls of butter in a saucepan with chopped herbs to taste, and simmer a few minutes. Add ⅓ cup of flour, stir well; add 1 cup of stock. Season to taste with salt and pepper. Add the chopped veal. Remove from fire and shape into balls. Let stand until cold. Dip into melted butter, then into crumbs, then into egg, again in crumbs. Then fry them. *Annette*

Braised Leg of Mutton

Bone a leg of mutton and lard it with fine strips of bacon. Rub with salt, pepper and any desired herbs, such as thyme. Put together with skewers so as to make it appear it is not boned. Put 3 tablespoonfuls of butter in a saucepan and brown the meat in this. When a good color, add 3 cups of stock, 3 carrots cut lengthwise in strips, 3 onions, each with a clove stuck in it, 3 sprigs of parsley and the bones of your leg of mutton. Cover and let simmer four hours. If the sauce is too thin when you go to serve it, thicken with a little flour. *Annette*

Hash of Braised or Roasted Leg of Mutton

Melt 3 tablespoonfuls of butter in a saucepan add 1 teaspoonful of shallot chopped fine and fry for five minutes over a low flame. Add 1 tablespoonful of flour, 1 cup of stock, ½ teaspoonful of salt and 1 teaspoonful of vinegar. Let it simmer for twenty minutes. Have 2 cups of mutton cut up in small pieces, very neat, and let them heat in your sauce without boiling.

Annette

Braised Mutton Chops

Melt 1 tablespoonful of butter in a frying pan. Put in 6 chops and brown lightly and quickly on both sides. Add 3 carrots cut lengthwise in strips, 6 very small onions, 3 of which should have a clove stuck in, 3 sprigs of parsley, and 1 cup of stock. Let simmer one hour. Serve with any sauce you like, such as sauce piquante, sauce soubise or tomato sauce.

Annette

Fricandeau

Take a nice piece of clear veal, and lard it well. Put into a saucepan 3 carrots cut round, 3 small onions cut in slices. Put your veal upon them and pour in stock until it comes halfway up the meat. Add 1 teaspoonful of salt and a few peppercorns. When it comes to a boil, put a sheet of buttered paper over it, cover closely, and let it simmer over a low flame for four hours. The fricandeau ought to be a good, brown color. Serve it with sorrel or endive or in its own sauce.

Annette

Veal Cutlets in Papers

Take 2 pounds of veal cutlet, in 2 cutlets, and flatten well.
Butter a sheet of paper, sprinkle with bread crumbs,
mushrooms, and herbs chopped very fine. Salt and pepper. Butter two other sheets of paper and put under the
first. Lay your cutlet on, twist your paper round in the
form of the piece and tie it with a short piece of thread.
Do the same with both cutlets. Put in a baking pan and
bake one hour in a moderate oven. When they are done,
remove outer paper.   *Annette*

Another Way

Take 6 lamb chops, put each in sheet of paper that has
been well buttered on the inside and dipped in water to
prevent burning. Season with salt, pepper, and bread
crumbs. Roll them in the papers to preserve the gravy,
tying the ends of the paper neatly. Bake in a moderate
oven three-quarters of an hour. Serve them in the papers.
                                                       Volney

Beef Olives

Take slices of round of beef, cut medium thick, about the
size of one's hand. Dip in egg, sprinkle with bread crumbs,
salt and pepper, roll them up and tie, or fasten with
skewers. Put in a pan and half-cover with stock. Add a
little nutmeg and 4 small onions. Stew for one hour, or
until tender.   *Scotch*

French Beefsteak

Cut 2 pounds of filet of beef into six pieces. Soak them in olive oil with salt in it for two hours. Put them on the broiler, under a hot flame, and broil ten minutes, turning once. Serve them with a maître d'hôtel sauce and surround with potatoes. The potatoes should be cut in pieces lengthwise, after they have been peeled, and fried in hot butter, turning them all the time that they may be equally brown on all sides. *Annette*

Larded Filet of Beef

Lard 3 pounds of tenderloin of beef. Put it in a deep dish, lay a bay leaf on it along with 3 sprigs of parsley and 3 sliced onions. Pour over it ¾ cup of olive oil mixed with ¼ cup of vinegar and let it soak for at least twenty-four hours. Pour the oil and vinegar frequently over the meat, with a spoon, while soaking. When ready to roast, remove from sauce, place on a rack in a roasting pan, sprinkle with salt and pepper and put in bottom of pan ¼ cupful of suet cut in small pieces. Put in hot oven and bake about thirty minutes. Baste three times during roasting. You may serve it either with or without sauce. If with sauce, you make use of the drippings of the beef to make a sauce piquante. *Annette*

French Roast Beef

Take a roast rib of beef weighing about 6 or 7 pounds and soak it in oil and vinegar as in the preceding recipe, keeping it in half as long again as the tender filet. Put it in a roasting pan, dust with salt, pepper and a little flour, and put in a hot oven. Roast one and a half hours, basting it four or five times. One-half cup of water may be added. Put on a platter and pour the gravy over it, having first skimmed off the grease.

Beef à la Mode

Take a pot roast weighing about five pounds and lard it well with bacon that you have first sprinkled with salt, pepper and any desired herbs, chopped fine. Put it in a pan (a Dutch oven is best), add 4 carrots cut in slices lengthwise, 4 small onions, 3 of which must each have a clove stuck in, a knuckle of veal, 4 sprigs of parsley and a cup of stock. Cover and let it cook slowly for four or five hours. The sauce ought to be thick. *Annette*

Beef à la Mode

Take 4 pounds of top of the round and cut off most of the fat. Mix together 1 onion chopped fine, 1 sprig of chopped parsley; ½ teaspoonful of salt, ¼ teaspoonful of pepper, ⅛ teaspoonful of grated nutmeg, and ¼ teaspoonful of thyme. Take 4 strips of lean bacon and the fat from the meat, roll in the above mixture and lard the meat with this. Put 4 pieces of bacon into the bottom of your pan (a Dutch oven is best), lay the beef on it and lay on the roast 4 or 5 more strips of bacon. Cut 3 small onions fine, slice 3 carrots, and put in the pot. Add salt and pepper, ¼ teaspoonful of grated nutmeg, a pinch of thyme, 1 wineglass of brandy and 1 glass of white wine. Put the pot on a low fire and let boil gently three hours, taking care that the meat does not stick to the bottom. Strain the gravy through a fine sieve, skim off the grease and serve.

Lemaire

Bouilli

Take 4 pounds of round of beef, put it in a soup kettle.
Pour on 4 quarts of cold water and bring to a boil. Skim
the foam as it rises. When the water boils add ½ cup cold
water to clear it. Skim again. When all scum has been removed set over a very low flame and let it stew gently.
Add 2 teaspoonfuls of salt, 8 peppercorns, 6 whole
cloves, 4 onions, 4 carrots, 4 turnips, 1 stalk of celery.
When they are tender remove and cut up fine to season
the soup.

While the beef is cooking make the glazing as follows:
Stew a knuckle of veal with a piece of bacon and the same
vegetables and seasoning used in the foregoing. When
the meat falls from the bone strain off the broth and simmer until it is of a consistency to coat a spoon when with-
drawn from it. Pour this over the boiled beef just before
serving. For the gravy, cream 2 tablespoonfuls of butter
with 1 of flour, add 1 pickled cucumber, minced, 1 anchovy, crushed, and 1 tablespoon of capers. Put in the
same saucepan in which the glazing was prepared. Add
¾ cupful of water, bring to a boil, stirring constantly.
Pour into sauce boat and serve at once. *Lemaire*

Beef à la Daube

Take 4 pounds of round of beef and lard it well. Put it in a Dutch oven. Cut the meat from a pound of shin of beef and cut in small pieces. Mix with it 1 cupful of veal or lamb, cut in small pieces, and ¼-pound of bacon cut up. Season the mixture with 1 teaspoonful of salt, ½ teaspoonful of pepper, ½ teaspoonful of dried thyme or a sprig of fresh, 3 carrots cut in slices and 2 onions, sliced. Put the seasoning around and over the beef. Cover with water. Let cook very slowly until tender. Remove beef and set aside to cool.

The jelly is now to be made. Remove all small pieces of meat, skim the grease off, and pass the gravy through a fine sieve. Put back on the fire and let simmer slowly with a few grains of pepper. Beat the whites of 5 eggs a very little with ½ cup of water. Pour into gravy, stir well for five minutes. Bring to a boil, then turn fire low and let simmer twenty minutes. Strain through a fine cheesecloth and you will have a clear jelly. When cool, cut into shapes and garnish the beef with it. This dish should be prepared the day before it is wanted. *Monticello*

To Stew Beef

Cut 2 pounds of the top of the round of beef into small cubes. Add 1 pint of white wine, half a grated nutmeg, 4 whole cloves, 8 peppercorns, 1 teaspoonful of salt, and a slice of ham cut into cubes. Let stew until the meat is tender. Half an hour before serving add 1 stalk of celery cut into fine pieces. *Monticello*

Minced Collops

Take 2 pounds of any tender cut of cooked beef. Cut into small cubes. Season with ½ teaspoonful of grated nutmeg, 1 teaspoonful of salt, ½ teaspoonful of pepper. Put into a pan with 1 shredded onion and 3 tablespoonfuls of butter. Turn all over and over until lightly browned. Add ½ cup of stock, 1 tablespoonful of catsup, 1 tablespoonful of chopped capers, and ½ cupful of sliced mushrooms. Thicken the gravy with 1 tablespoonful of flour mixed with an equal amount of butter. Garnish your dish with forcemeat balls and pickles.   *Monticello*

Forcemeat

One-half pound of lean bacon, ½ pound of suet, chop both fine. Add ½ teaspoonful of sweet herbs, shred fine, ⅛ teaspoonful of powdered mace, nutmeg, pepper and salt. Add the yolks of 2 eggs and beat all well together.

Monticello

Breast of Mutton

Manage it as you did the bouilli. When done season it with salt, pepper and nutmeg to taste. For gravy melt 3 tablespoonfuls of butter, add gradually 2 of grated bread crumbs. Stir until brown. Add ¼ cupful of the juice of the meat.   *Lemaire*

Potted Beef

Take 3 pounds of shin of beef. Cut in very small pieces.
Put in a pot with the bone, barely cover with water and
cook until tender. Set aside to cool. Remove fat. Heat
it again, remove bones, and chop meat as fine as for
mincemeat. Add to it all the remaining gravy, season to
taste with salt, pepper and any desired spices. Turn into
moulds.   *Mrs. Calver*

Stew Made of Cold Meat

Slice your meat, put it in a pan with 2 large spoonfuls of
water, ¼ teaspoonful of pepper and salt. Just before serving add 3 tablespoonfuls of butter, 2 tablespoonfuls of
walnut catsup, 2 of currant jelly, 1 teaspoonful of mustard. Let heat thoroughly, and serve.   *Edgehill*

Boeuf à la Mode

Take 4 pounds of round of beef, lard well and season with
1 teaspoonful of salt; ½ teaspoonful of pepper, 1 bay leaf.
Put it into a pot, brown well, add 1 glass of wine and the
juice of a lemon. Let simmer until tender.

Dictionaire de la cuisine

Boeuf Bouilli à l'Oddette

Melt 3 tablespoonfuls of butter, add ½ pound of sliced
mushrooms. Sprinkle over all 2 tablespoonfuls of flour
and stir well. Pour on 1½ cups of stock, add 1 small
onion with a clove stuck in it. Let simmer ten minutes.
Add 2 cups of boiled beef cut in small slices. Ladle gravy
over all thoroughly. Bring to boiling point. Add the yolk
of 1 egg and 1 teaspoonful of vinegar or lemon. Put on a
platter. Surround with croutons. Serve.   *Baron de Brise*

Beef Olives

Put 1 pound of beef through the food chopper. Add an equal quantity of boiled rice. Season with salt and pepper and stir in 1 egg. Form into small balls and put in a hot oven for twenty minutes.

Septimia Randolph Meikelham's cook, Nancy

Chicken Pudding No. 1

Disjoint 2 chickens and parboil them. Butter a baking dish and lay the chickens in, dot with butter, season with pepper and salt. Beat 4 eggs until light, add 1 cup of milk, 1 cup of flour, 1 scant teaspoonful baking powder; ½ teaspoonful of salt. Pour over the chicken and bake in a moderate oven for one hour. *Mrs. Elizabeth Lea*

Chicken Pudding No. 2

Disjoint 2 young chickens, dust with salt and pepper. Take 1 quart of potatoes, wash and peel them. Cut in slices, boil until tender and mash them. Add 2 tablespoonfuls of butter, salt and pepper to taste, and 1 pint of milk. Put a layer of this in the bottom of a glass baking dish, then a layer of chicken, and so on until the dish is full. Bake one hour in a moderate oven.

Cold Fresh Meat

Cut any cold, roasted meat in thin slices. Chop fine 2 sprigs of parsley, 1 of thyme, and 3 spears of chives. Mix with 6 tablespoonfuls of bread crumbs, ½ teaspoonful of salt, ¼ teaspoonful of pepper. Sprinkle over the meat, and pour over all ½ cup of French dressing.

Filet of Veal with Madeira Sauce

Take 3 pounds of clear veal, lard with pork, place in a saucepan with 2 tablespoonfuls of butter, 3 carrots cut in slices, 2 sliced onions, a sprig of thyme, 1 bay leaf, and 1 cup of stock. Season with salt and pepper. Cover, and simmer until tender. Serve with a sauce made of the gravy of the meat to which add ½ cup of sliced mushrooms, any desired seasoning and 1 wineglass of Madeira wine.

Blanquette of Veal

Cut 3 pounds of the breast of veal in pieces 1 inch long. Soak in cold water for two hours. Drain and wipe dry. Melt 4 tablespoonfuls of butter and brown the veal in this. Season with salt and pepper, cover with stock, and stew until tender. *Professor Blot*

Beefsteak Pie

Cut 2 pounds of beefsteak into small pieces. Stew in a little water until half done. Season with salt and pepper. Line a baking dish with puff paste, put in the steak. Season the gravy very high and pour in the dish. Cover with paste and bake until the paste is a nice brown.

Mrs. Mary Randolph

Veal Cutlets

Take 2 pounds of veal cutlets cut in two slices. Lay in a pan
with ¼ pound of pork, a clove of garlic, a sprig of thyme,
and 2 of parsley. Cover with water and simmer for fifteen
minutes. Remove meat from pan, lay on a dish and let
cool. When cold, cover well with sifted bread crumbs
mixed with chopped parsley, pepper, salt, and grated nutmeg. Press firmly on veal with a broad knife. When a little
dried, turn meat and do the same to other side.

Put 4 tablespoonfuls of lard or other fat in a frying
pan. When it starts to smoke drop cutlets in. Brown on
both sides. Meanwhile simmer the water in which the
veal was cooked until it is reduced to one cupful. Strain it
and thicken with 1 tablespoonful of butter mixed with 1
tablespoonful of flour. Add ½ cup of wine, ¼ cup of
mushroom catsup, put in the cutlets and stew until tender. Serve with forcemeat balls.   *Mrs. Mary Randolph*

Pie of Sweetbreads and Oysters

Drop a sweetbread into acidulated salted boiling water
and cook slowly for twenty minutes. Plunge into cold
water. Drain and cut in cubes. Stew a pint of oysters until
the edges curl. Add 2 tablespoonfuls of butter creamed
with 1 tablespoonful of flour, 1 cup of cream and the
yolks of 3 eggs well beaten. Season with salt and pepper
to taste. Line a deep baking dish with puff paste. Put in a
layer of oysters, then a layer of sweetbreads until the dish
is nearly full. Pour the sauce over all and put a crust on
top. Bake until the paste is a delicate brown. This is the
most delicate pie that can be made.

Boiled Leg of Mutton

Dredge a leg of mutton with flour and put in a kettle. Cover with cold water. Add 2 teaspoonfuls of salt, 1 small garlic, which will give it a delicately fine flavor. Bring to a boil. Skim well. When tender remove from broth and cover to keep hot. Have ready 6 carrots cut in slices and cooked, 4 turnips boiled and mashed with a lump of butter. Salt and pepper. Lay the mutton on this. Melt 4 tablespoonfuls of butter, add 1 tablespoonful of flour, 4 tablespoonfuls of capers with some of the vinegar in which they came. Mix all well together and spread over the mutton. *Mrs. Mary Randolph*

Haricot of Mutton

Take a rack of mutton, separate into chops, beat flat, sprinkle with salt and pepper and broil until a pale brown. Stew the trimmings with 2 cups of water, strain, season well with salt, pepper, a pinch of thyme, and any preferred catsup. Simmer until reduced by one-half. Thicken with 1 tablespoonful of butter rolled in flour. Have ready 4 carrots and 2 turnips cut into small dice and boiled until tender. Put in the gravy, heat all well, and serve.

Mrs. Mary Randolph

Mutton Chops

Cut a rack of mutton as for haricot. Stew in 2 cups of water, 1 teaspoonful of salt, ¼ teaspoonful of pepper, until tender. Prepare a gravy with 1 tablespoonful of butter, 2 tablespoonfuls boiling water, 1 tablespoonful of mushroom catsup, ½ teaspoonful of salt. Stir thoroughly and pour over the meat. *Mrs. Mary Randolph*

To Boil a Ham

Ham should be washed and soaked all night in cold water. The next morning scrape and wash well, put on to boil in water to cover it more than well. Boil for five, six, or seven hours. It is not done until the bone in the under part comes off with ease. But it is best not to boil it until the meat is in strings. *Monticello*

Hams improve in flavor until they are two years old. After that they are neither better nor worse. *Monticello*

Ham with Bread Crumbs

This is always done in the hams of the first year. Boil as in the preceding receipt and remove the skin. Cover the top slightly with bread crumbs and put in the oven until of a light brown. *Monticello*

Glazed Ham

Take the skin off of the boiled ham—old ham—and let it get cold. Sprinkle it thick with sugar. Set under a broiler and glaze it well. *Monticello*

Boiled Turkey with Oyster Sauce

Grate a loaf of bread, chop a dozen large oysters fine, add ¼ teaspoonful of nutmeg, ½ teaspoonful of salt, ½ teaspoonful of pepper. Mix into a light forcemeat with ¼ pound of butter, 2 tablespoonfuls of cream and 3 eggs. Stuff the turkey, making any remaining into balls and boil them. Sew up the turkey, dredge with flour, and put in a kettle with enough cold water to cover well. Set over a medium fire. As the scum begins to rise, remove it. Let it boil very slowly one hour. Remove kettle from heat and keep closely covered another hour. The steam being kept in will stew it enough, make it rise, keep the skin whole, tender and very white. When you serve it, pour on a little oyster sauce, lay the balls around and serve the rest of the sauce in a boat. Put it on the fire to heat just before serving. *Mrs. Mary Randolph*

Sauce for the Turkey

Drain 1 pint of oysters. Add the juice to 1 cupful of cream sauce. Add 1 teaspoonful of lemon pickle, 1 tablespoonful of butter mixed with 1 tablespoonful of flour and 1 tablespoonful of cream. Add the oysters and stir until they are hot, but do not boil for it will make them hard and appear small. *Mrs. Mary Randolph*

Turkey à la Daube

Bone a small turkey. Put pepper and salt on the inside and cover with slices of ham or boiled tongue. Fill it with a seasoned forcemeat. Sew it up and boil gently until tender. Cover it with jelly and serve. *Mrs. Mary Randolph*

Roasted Goose

Chop a few sage leaves and 2 onions very fine, mix with 2 tablespoonfuls of butter, 1 teaspoonful of pepper, 2 teaspoonfuls of salt. Put it in the goose. Rub over with butter, dredge with flour, and put in a hot oven. Baste with melted butter. Roast one and one-half hours. Add ½ cup boiling water to the gravy.   *Mrs. Mary Randolph*

Sauce for a Goose

Pare, core and slice 6 apples. Put them in a saucepan with just enough water to prevent them from sticking. Set over a very slow fire and cook until reduced to a pulp. Add 1 tablespoonful of butter, sugar to taste and beat well.

Mrs. Mary Randolph

Roasted Ducks

Shred 1 onion and a few sage leaves fine. Put them in the duck with ½ teaspoonful of salt and ½ teaspoonful of pepper. Dust with flour and put in a hot oven. Baste with melted butter. If your oven is very hot it will roast in half an hour. The quicker it is roasted the better it will taste. Prepare a gravy with the broth from the gizzard, liver and heart which have been stewed. Into the broth put a large blade of mace, four peppercorns, 1 tablespoonful of catsup, 1 teaspoonful of lemon pickle. Strain and pour it on the ducks. Serve onion sauce in a boat.

Mrs. Mary Randolph

Roasted Wild Ducks or Teal

Put into each of your ducks a small onion, ½ teaspoonful of salt, ¼ teaspoonful of pepper and 1 tablespoonful of red wine. Put in a very hot oven and roast twenty minutes. Make a gravy of the necks and gizzards, 1 tablespoonful of red wine, half an anchovy, a blade of mace, 1 onion, salt and a dash of cayenne pepper. Cook in 2 cups of water and simmer until reduced to 1 cup. Strain through a fine sieve and pour over the ducks. Serve with onion sauce in a boat.

Mrs. Mary Randolph

Chicken Pie

Boil 2 young chickens in salted water barely to cover them for one-half hour. Have a sprig of parsley, a few celery leaves and 2 whole cloves in the water. Cut them in small pieces, removing all skin. Have a deep dish lined with pastry, already baked. Put in a layer of chicken, sprinkle with flour, salt, pepper, a little mace and some of the chopped hearts and livers. Continue until dish is full. Pour in as much of the liquor in which the chickens were cooked as the dish will hold. Wet the edges of the pastry with water, lay on the top crust, close the edges carefully, prick well, and bake until the top crust is done. The crust for a chicken pie should be thicker than for a fruit pie.

Mrs. Horace Mann

Fried Chicken

Disjoint 2 young chickens. Dredge the pieces well with flour, sprinkle with salt and pepper and drop into deep fat. Fry until a golden brown. Brown small circles of cold mush (corn meal boiled in water with salt and poured in a pan until cold), and fry a dozen sprigs of parsley, to garnish the dish. Scald 1 cup of cream, add 1 tablespoonful of butter, salt and pepper to taste, and 1 teaspoonful of chopped parsley. Pour over the chickens and serve.

Mrs. Mary Randolph

Venison

Lard well a saddle of venison, dust with salt and pepper. Put in a hot oven. Baste with cream, as it is not very fat. Serve with currant jelly sauce. *Mrs. Horace Mann*

FISH

How to Ascertain if Fish Whether Boiled, Stewed, or Fried, is Done

If the bone sticks firm to the flesh, or the flesh to the bone, it is not done. By the same rule, if quite loose, and the flesh of the fish drops off the bone, it is overdone, and you lose some of its qualities. For fish in slices, try the bone with your knife; if the flesh comes from it, it is done; or by placing the point of a knife between the flesh and the bone, and on raising it, if done, the knife will part it easily.

To boil a large fish whole it is requisite to have a drain at the bottom of the kettle. *Soyer*

New Way of Boiling Fish

The addition of a few herbs and vegetables in the water gives a very nice flavor to the fish. Add, according to taste, half a sliced onion, a sprig of thyme, a bay leaf, winter savory, 2 carrots, a stalk of celery, 3 or 4 whole cloves, a blade of mace, using whichever of the ingredients you have at hand.

Fresh water fish, which have no particular flavor, are preferable done thus, with the addition of a little vinegar.

Soyer

Baked Fish

Wash well a sole, or other fish, and dry thoroughly. Chop fine 1 onion and 4 or 5 sprigs of parsley. Put 2 tablespoonfuls of melted butter in your baking pan. Sprinkle some of the chopped onion and parsley on it and lay the fish on this. Season with salt and pepper. Mix the remainder of the chopped onion and parsley with bread crumbs, about ¾ cup more or less according to size of fish. Dot over with butter and pour a glass of wine or broth in the pan. Bake until done. A large sole will require about an hour. If necessary, put under the broiler a few moments to brown nicely.

Soyer

Remains of Boiled Fish

The remains of boiled fish may always be prepared as above. A few spoonfuls of melted butter poured over the fish before strewing on the crumbs makes it more delicate.

Soyer

To Dress Codfish No. 1

Boil your fish in salted water until tender. Scald 1 cup of milk and 1 cup of cream with 2 tablespoonfuls of butter. Shred your fish fine and put it in this gravy. Simmer for fifteen minutes. Add 4 hard-boiled eggs chopped fine and a good dash of nutmeg. Put on a platter, cover with the yolks of 2 hard-boiled eggs pressed through a sieve, and serve.   *Monticello*

Fish with Potatoes

Boil and shred your fish. Have ready some mashed potatoes. Mix them, in equal quantities, with 2 tablespoonfuls of butter, ¼ teaspoonful of grated nutmeg, ⅛ teaspoonful of pepper, ½ teaspoonful of salt, and 2 tablespoonfuls of brandy. Beat well. If too stiff, add more cream or milk. Turn into a dish lined with piecrust and bake until set.

Martha Jefferson Randolph

To Fry Fish

The great art in frying fish is to have it free from grease. It is important to have plenty of fat in the pan and to have it very hot. If at the proper degree of temperature, a sole and an apple fritter may be fried in the same pan, without either tasting of the other. To ascertain the proper degree of heat put a cube of bread in the fat. If it hisses, the fat is ready. If the bread burns, it is too hot. If the bread is a delicate brown, the fat is just right. The fish should be dipped in egg, then in bread crumbs with which salt and pepper have been mixed. Shake off all loose crumbs before putting in pan. Turn once while frying.   *Soyer*

Oyster Pie

Line a dish with pastry and bake it. Take 1 quart of oysters, put the juice in a saucepan with ½ teaspoonful of mace, a glass of wine, the juice of 1 lemon, and bring to a boil. Pour in 1 cup of cream and thicken the gravy with 2 scant tablespoonfuls of flour mixed with 2 tablespoonfuls of butter. Add the oysters and bring to a boil. Pour into the prepared crust. The upper crust should have been baked separately on a baking sheet and laid on top of the pie after the oysters are put in.   *Mrs. Horace Mann*

Tongues and Sounds

The principal thing to be observed in dressing tongues and sounds is to freshen them as much as possible by washing and soaking. When all possible salt has been removed they should be boiled until thoroughly done. They may be served plain or with any desired sauce, or they may be mixed with enough melted butter, pepper, and chopped parsley to form a sauce for them.

Broiled Shad

Separate one side from the backbone so that it will lie open without being split in two. Wash thoroughly, dry with a clean cloth and sprinkle with salt and pepper. Let it stand until you are ready to broil it. Put under a hot broiler, broil until a nice brown. Pour melted butter over it and serve.   *Mrs. Mary Randolph*

Fried Fish, Jewish Fashion

Take a pound piece of halibut, lay in a dish. Sprinkle salt on the top and put some water in the dish, about half way up the fish. Let stand one hour. Take it out, dry it, cut out the bones. It is then in two pieces. Lay the pieces on their side and cut in slices one-half inch thick. Put ¼ pound of any desired fat in a frying pan. Mix 4 table-spoonfuls of flour with 1 egg and a little water to form a smooth batter, not too thick. Dip the fish in this, until well covered, drop in the hot fat and fry to a golden brown. Drain in brown paper, put on platter and serve. Any desired sauce may be used, but plain, with salt and lemon is usual. Other fish may be done in this way.

Soyer

Boiled Rockfish

The best part of the rock is the head and shoulders. Put it into a fish kettle with enough water to cover and 1 tea-spoonful of salt. Boil gently and skim well. When tender drain off the water and lay the fish on a platter. Garnish with grated horseradish. Serve with melted butter mixed with chopped parsley or, for a change, with anchovy butter. The roe and liver should be fried and served sepa-rately.

Mrs. Mary Randolph

Fried Perch

Clean the fish well but do not remove the roes. Dry, sprinkle with salt and pepper and dredge with flour. Lay them on a board. When one side is dry, turn, sprinkle other side with salt, pepper and flour. Drop into hot fat and fry until a golden brown. It takes about five minutes. Serve with melted butter or anchovy sauce.

Mrs. Mary Randolph

VEGETABLES

Dressing Vegetables

Lard is even better than butter for frying vegetables, but must be kept at a high temperature or the vegetables will taste of it.

Salsify

Salsify must be scraped and not prepared until it is time to cook it or it will turn dark.

One way to dress salsify is to boil it after it is scraped. When tender, mash and fry in little cakes the size of sausages. Another way is to scrape and cut in small pieces the size of dice. Boil until tender. Put in a pan with a lump of butter, a little milk, flour, or bread crumbs, pepper and salt, and stew for twenty minutes.

Third way for salsify. Scrape, cut it lengthwise, and fry it.

Turnips

Peel and boil until tender as many turnips as desired. Mash through a colander. Add butter, salt, pepper and a little milk, and stew for fifteen minutes so as to dry them.

With sugar. Peel turnips, cut in pieces and put them in a vessel with a spoonful of butter, half a cup of brown sugar and a pint of hot water. Stew until tender.

At Monticello we used to have turnips dressed with cheese.

Polenta

Make mush (corn meal boiled in salt water, slowly, until thick) and turn into a square pan. When cold, cut in thin slices and lay in a baking dish, grate cheese over the mush, and dot with butter. Repeat these layers, letting a layer of cheese and butter be on top, until the dish is full. Bake in a moderate oven until the cheese is thoroughly melted.

Macaroni

Break macaroni in small pieces, there should be 2 cupfuls, and boil in salted water until tender. Grate ¼ pound of cheese and mix with the same amount of butter. Stir into macaroni and bake like polenta.

Potatoes

Potatoes may be wrung in a cloth after they are boiled. This is good when they are small or indifferent. When they are small, several can be wrung together.

They may be mashed, with milk and butter added after they are boiled. Serve them thus, or form into cakes, and fry like salsify.

Carthusian

Cut a head of Savoy cabbage in 4 pieces, wash well. Put in an iron pot with 3 quarts of water and boil for fifteen minutes. Drain in a colander and press out all the water. Remove the stalk from each piece and chop, not too fine. The monks always had a foundation of cabbage, or of greens, or of Brussels sprouts, one pound of either, prepared as above. Then they added 1 pound either of boiled carrots, turnips, parsnips, beets, artichokes, potatoes, leeks, celery or onions. Boil the pound of whatever you choose from the above until tender. Chop it as you did the cabbage, adding ½ teaspoonful of salt. Take 3 medium-sized pigs' tongues, which should have been boiled with the cabbage, cut them through lengthwise. Line your pan on the bottom and around the sides with the chopped vegetables, about an inch deep. Place the meat in the center, thus making it invisible when turned out. When filled add ¼ pound of butter, 1 wineglassful of vinegar, and ½ cup of water. Cover and set upon a very slow fire for two hours. Then drain all the gravy into a bowl. Run a knife around the pot, put platter over the pan, reverse, turn out, and your Carthusian will appear as a pudding. Pour the gravy, or bread-crumb sauce over it and serve.

You may also, for a change, pour a little white or brown sauce over it, but take care that the vegetables must always be kept firm enough to turn out like a pudding.

Soyer

For Vegetarians

The foregoing will, by omitting the meat, be applicable to vegetarians.

Parsnips

Parsnips may be cooked, mashed and fried in cakes like salsify.

How It May Be Varied

Instead of tongue you may use pigs' feet, pickled pork, bacon, ham, liver of all kinds, previously fried, or partly so; sausages, salt beef, previously boiled and cut in slices, or any part of fresh meats previously roasted and cut in slices. Pigeons or partridges and all kinds of small birds may be put in rows, only they should be larded and stuffed previously.

Soyer

Chartreuse

At Monticello the vegetables, all roots, no cabbage, were cut in slices and arranged in a fanciful way, alternating carrots with white vegetables, in a mould with straight sides. The mould was filled with forcemeat balls. It turned out in a beautiful form and made a very pretty dish for a ceremonious dinner.

Monticello

Podrilla à la Creole

Put 1 pint of red beans to soak the night before. Drain in the morning. Cover with water, and set on the fire. Add ¼ pound salt pork cut into cubes. Season with salt and pepper to taste, add a bunch of herbs, bring to a boil and let cook very slowly until tender.

Wash 1 cup of rice well and boil in salted water until light and tender. Add 2 tablespoonfuls of butter, salt and pepper to taste. Press into a ring mould set in moderate oven for ten minutes. Turn out and fill the center with the beans which have been drained and from which the herbs have been removed.

Baron de Brise

PUDDINGS

South Carolina Rice Pudding

Beat the yolks of 5 eggs, add gradually 4 tablespoonfuls of sugar, and 1 pint of milk. Beat the whites of the eggs until stiff and mix with the yolks. Stir 2 tablespoonfuls of melted butter into ¾ cup of rice. Put into a baking dish and add about half the egg, a pinch of salt and milk mixture. Stir well. Pour the rest of the first mixture over it, add a piece of stick cinnamon, and bake in a moderate oven until set.   *Mrs. Allston*

Gâteau au Riz

Wash 6 tablespoonfuls of rice in several waters. Put in a saucepan and pour on 4 cups of milk. Cook until the rice is puffed and tender. Sweeten to taste and set aside to cool. When quite cold add the yolks of 4 eggs, and the grated rind of ½ lemon. Beat the whites to a froth and add to the rice. Butter a mould and dust with bread crumbs. Pour the rice mixture into the mould, set in a pan of water and bake one-half hour. Serve with the following sauce.   *Annette*

Sauce for Above

Bring 1½ cups of milk to a boil. Beat the yolks of 2 eggs until light, add 3 tablespoonfuls of sugar, ½ tablespoonful of flour, a pinch of salt. Simmer, stirring constantly, until slightly thick. Strain, let cool, add ½ teaspoonful of vanilla extract.

Annette

Philadelphia Pudding

Wash 1 cupful of rice well and stir it into 3 pints of milk. Sweeten to taste, add pinch of salt, and flavor with nutmeg, vanilla, or cinnamon. When all is mixed set over a very low flame for five or six hours. It must not be stirred or put over too hot a fire.

Virginia Randolph Trist

Indian Pudding No. 1

Chop fine ½ pound of suet. Mix with ½ cup of corn meal, 1 cup of molasses, ¼ teaspoonful of salt, and 1 quart of milk. Stir well and pour into baking dish. Set in a slow oven. As it bakes, add more milk to prevent it thickening and hardening. Two hours will bake it. It is eaten with butter and sugar, or molasses.

Boston

Indian Meal Pudding No. 2

Mix 8 tablespoonfuls of meal with 1 cup of molasses, add 2 tablespoonfuls of melted butter, and ¼ teaspoonful of salt. Beat 2 eggs light and stir in first mixture. Add slowly 1 quart of milk that has been brought to a boil. Bake for two hours in a slow oven.

Boiled Loaf

Cut the crust off a loaf of bread and put it in a deep dish. Pour 1 cupful of milk over it and let it soak thoroughly. Then boil it in water to cover, but not long enough for it to fall to pieces. It should preserve the form of the loaf. Serve with any preferred sauce. *Monticello*

Bread Pudding No. 1

Cut the crusts off a loaf of bread and slice the bread into a deep dish. Pour 1 quart of scalded milk over it and let it soak an hour. Stir until the lumps are all dissolved. Beat 5 eggs until very light. Add to first mixture, with ½ cup of sugar and ¼ teaspoonful of salt. Take a square pudding cloth, dip in cold water, wring out and dust well with flour. Pour the pudding into this, tie tightly, and boil for two hours. *Ellen Randolph Coolidge*

Sauce for the Above

Mix 1 cup of sugar with 1 tablespoonful of flour and a pinch of salt. Add the juice and rind of 1 lemon and 1 cup of boiling water. Add 2 tablespoonfuls of butter, simmer for five minutes, strain and serve. *Ellen Randolph Coolidge*

Bread Pudding No. 2

Remove the crusts from a loaf of bread and crumble the bread fine. Add it to a quart of milk, bring to a boil and let simmer for fifteen minutes. Beat the yolks of 6 eggs and the whites of 3 until light. Add 6 tablespoonfuls of sugar, ¼ teaspoonful of salt and the grated rind of 1 lemon. Beat all well together and bake in a moderate oven for three-quarters of an hour.

Sauce

Melt 2 tablespoonfuls of butter, add 2 of brandy, 1 cupful of sugar mixed with 1 teaspoonful of flour. Stir over a slow fire until it thickens.   *Martha Jefferson Randolph*

Bread and Butter Pudding

Cut a stale, square loaf of bread in slices and spread each slice with a thick layer of butter. Take a deep baking dish, cover the bottom with bread, strew in a few currants or stoned raisins, then another layer of bread, and so on until the dish is two-thirds full. Beat 6 eggs, add 1 cupful of sugar, 4 cups of milk, and any kind of seasoning that is preferred. Pour this into the dish and let stand two hours. Bake one and one-half hours in a slow oven.   *Mrs. Putnam*

Batter Pudding No. 1

Mix 3 tablespoonfuls of flour with ¼ teaspoonful of salt and a little grated nutmeg. Stir into this 2 cups of milk and cook until it thickens. Add 4 tablespoonfuls of butter and let cool. When cold, add 6 well-beaten eggs. Beat all together thoroughly. Butter a mould, pour in the pudding, cover, and boil for two and one-half hours. Serve with wine sauce.

Batter Pudding No. 2

Beat 6 eggs, add 4 cups milk, ¼ teaspoonful of salt and enough flour to make a thin batter. Grease a baking dish well, pour your pudding in and bake in a very hot oven. One-half hour should bake it.   *Harriet Douglas*

Corn Pudding

Grate 6 ears of green corn. Mix with it ½ cup of cream,
2 eggs, a tablespoonful of butter, ½ tablespoonful of sugar
and a sprinkle of salt. Mix all well together and bake.

Mrs. Derby, Newport

Gâteau de Pomme de Terre

Peel 6 large potatoes, cut them up and place in a saucepan. Cover with water and boil until tender. Drain and
press them through a colander. Add the well-beaten yolks
of 3 eggs, and sugar to taste. Beat the whites of the eggs
to a stiff froth and fold them into the first mixture. Butter
a mould well and dust with bread crumbs. Pour in the
pudding and bake in a moderate oven until set, from one-
half to three-quarters of an hour.

Annette

Laid Pudding

Remove the crusts from a loaf of bread, slice the bread
and lay to soak in 2 cups of scalded milk. Put a layer of
the bread in a baking dish, sprinkle with a layer of currants. Alternate bread and currants until the dish is nearly
full. Pour in 2 cups of milk and 2 cups of cream, mixed
and sweetened to taste. Add ¼ cup of brandy, ¼ cup of
wine, ½ cup of almonds blanched and chopped fine, and 1
tablespoonful of candied orange or lemon peel, finely
chopped, also ⅛ teaspoonful of nutmeg, of cloves and of
mace. Bake the pudding in a moderate oven until set.
Serve with melted butter, wine and sugar.

English

Proportions of a Plum Pudding

Mix together 1 pound of chopped suet, 4 tablespoonfuls of brown sugar, ½ pound of currants, 1 pound of raisins, 3 tablespoonfuls of flour, 4 cups of grated bread crumbs, 12 eggs, 1 grated nutmeg, 1 teaspoonful of cinnamon, 1 of mace, 1 tablespoonful of finely cut citron, 1 teaspoonful of salt, and 1 wineglass of brandy.

Wyeth's English Plum Pudding

Two pounds of best seedless raisins, 1 pound currants, 1 pound sultana raisins, 1 quart grated bread crumbs, 1 quart beef suet chopped fine, ½ pound citron cut fine, 2 ounces candied orange peel, 2 ounces candied lemon peel cut fine, 1 grated nutmeg, 1 teaspoonful of ginger, 1 of salt. Mix all well together. Beat 12 eggs and stir into the first mixture. Add 1 cup of brandy. If not moist enough add as much milk as will make it cling together. Put into tin forms and boil four or five hours. The water must be boiling when the pudding is put in. Plunge into cold water for a few minutes before turning out the pudding.

Plain Plum Pudding

Chop fine 1 cup of suet, mix in 1½ cups of sugar, 3 cups flour, ½ cup molasses, 2 cups raisins, 1 cup currants, 1 teaspoonful of soda dissolved in 1 tablespoonful of hot water and added to 1 cup of milk. Dip a cloth in boiling water, dredge it with flour, tie the pudding in it. Drop in boiling water and boil for two and one-half hours. Serve with any desired warm sauce. *Sarah Buckley*

Cheese Curd Pudding

Mix 2 quarts of milk with 1 pint of white wine and heat.
Drain all the curd from the whey. Put it in a bowl with ½
cup unsalted butter and beat curd and butter together
until well mixed. Beat the yolks of 3 eggs and the whites
of 2 and add to the curd. Stir in ½ cup of fine cake
crumbs. Sweeten to taste and add a pinch of salt. Butter
a baking dish and turn mixture into it. Bake in a slow
oven until set. Serve with melted butter, wine and sugar.

Martha Jefferson Randolph

Apple Pudding

Peel and boil until tender 3 or 4 apples. Press through a
sieve. To 1 cup of the purée add ½ cup of cream and
butter. Let cool. Add 3 well-beaten eggs, ½ cup of powdered sugar, the rind of 1 lemon. Mix all well together
and put in a crust. Half an hour will bake it.   *Monticello*

This pudding is made with either fresh or dried apples.

Curate Pudding

Four eggs, their weight in flour, the weight of 3 eggs in
sugar. Cream the butter, add sugar gradually and stir until a smooth paste. Separate the eggs. Mix the yolks with
the sugar and butter, then add flour, and stiffly beaten
egg whites, alternately, along with a pinch of salt. Put in
a mould, tie a cloth over top of mould and set in a pan of
boiling water. Let the water come halfway up the mould.
Renew as it boils away. Steam for two hours.

Mrs. Cox, Manhasset

Lemon Pudding No. 1

Beat the yolks of 4 eggs until very light. Cream ¼ cup of butter with 1 cup of sugar. Stir the yolks into this very gradually. Add the juice of 3 lemons and the grated rind of 1; also a pinch of salt. Put in a double boiler and cook until it thickens, stirring constantly. Have ready muffin pans lined with pastry. Pour the lemon mixture into them and bake in a moderate oven until done. Try with a straw; if the straw comes out clean, it is done.

Martha Jefferson Randolph

Lemon Pudding No. 2

Cream 1 cup of butter with 1 cup of sugar. Beat the yolks of 6 eggs until light. Add the juice and grated rind of 2 lemons. Combine mixtures and beat together until very light, add a pinch of salt. Pour into a baking dish lined with puff paste and bake three-quarters of an hour in a moderate oven.

If the butter and sugar are melted together and the eggs added while warm, it will make a transparent pudding.

Philadelphia

Lemon Pudding No. 3

Beat 6 eggs until very light. Add 1½ cups of sugar, ¼ cup melted butter, the juice and rind of 2 lemons, and a pinch of salt. Pour into a baking pan lined with pastry and bake until set.

Mrs. Fairfax

Molasses and Bread Pudding

Cut slices of bread, butter them well and lay in a pudding dish. Pour a layer of molasses over them. Do this until your dish is full. Set in a *very slow* oven and let it cook gradually for an hour or more. Set under broiler to brown before serving.   *Mrs. Beverly Randolph*

Apple Pudding

Pare and chop 8 apples. Butter a pudding dish and dust with bread crumbs and a layer of brown sugar. Add a layer of the apples, dot over with 1 tablespoonful of chopped citron and spices to taste. Repeat the crumbs, sugar, apples, spices and citron until your dish is full. Dot over with butter and bake one hour in a moderate oven.

Miss Martin

Sago Pudding No. 1

Scald 3 cups of milk with a piece of stick cinnamon, a piece of lemon rind and a dash of nutmeg. Add 3 tablespoonfuls of sago and cook until clear. Beat 4 eggs with 6 tablespoonfuls of sugar and a pinch of salt, add to first mixture. Remove cinnamon and lemon peel. Pour into a dish lined with pastry and bake until set.   *Domestic Cookery*

Sago Pudding No. 2

Scald 4 cups of milk with a piece of stick cinnamon. Add 8 tablespoonfuls of sago. Stir often. When thick, remove cinnamon; add 1 cup of butter, 1 cup of sugar, ½ cup of wine, and a pinch of salt. When cold add 6 well-beaten eggs and ½ cup of currants that have been soaked in hot water. Turn into a baking pan lined with pastry and bake until set. *Mrs. Mary Randolph*

Almond Pudding

Put ½ pound of blanched almonds through the food chopper, using finest grinder. Warm slightly 2 tablespoonfuls of cream and add ½ cup of butter. When melted stir into the almonds. Add 1 tablespoonful of brandy, a pinch of salt, a dash of nutmeg and sugar to taste. Butter custard cups, fill half full, set in a pan of water and bake until set. Serve with butter, wine and sugar. *Domestic Cookery*

Bread and Butter Pudding No. 2

Slice some bread, spread well with butter and lay in a baking dish with currants and sliced citron and lemon or orange peel between each layer of bread. Pour over this an unboiled custard made by beating 3 eggs, adding 2 cups of milk, 3 tablespoonfuls of sugar, a pinch of salt. Let stand two hours. Bake in a slow oven one hour.

A rim of pastry around the edge makes all puddings look better, but is not necessary. *Domestic Cookery*

Orange Pudding

Cream ¼ cup butter, add the grated rind of 1 orange and
1 cup of sugar. Beat until very light. Add 6 eggs well
beaten. Grate a raw apple and add to first mixture. Line
the bottom and sides of a pie plate with pastry. Pour in
the orange mixture and over it put crossbars of pastry.
Bake half an hour.   *Domestic Cookery*

Brown Bread Pudding

One-half pound of brown bread, grated, ½ pound of currants, ½ pound of chopped suet. Add 1 cup of sugar and
½ grated nutmeg. Mix in 4 well-beaten eggs, 1 tablespoonful of brandy and 2 tablespoonfuls of cream. Pour
into a well-buttered mould, or a pudding cloth, and boil
from three to four hours.   *Domestic Cookery*

Tapioca Pudding

Add 1 cup of tapioca to 2 cups of milk and set over a very
slow fire to swell. Stir often. Add 1 pint of cold milk, the
yolks of 4 eggs, 1½ cups of sugar, spice, or flavoring to
suit taste, 1 cup of currants and 1 cup of raisins. Bake one
hour in a slow oven.   *Mrs. Putnam*

Sweet Potato Pudding No. 1

Boil 1 pound of sweet potatoes until tender. Rub them
through a sieve. Add 5 well-beaten eggs, 1½ cups of
sugar, 1 cup of butter, the grated rind of 1 lemon, a dash
of nutmeg, and a wineglass of brandy. Line a baking dish
with pastry and pour in the mixture. Sprinkle with sugar
and bits of citron and bake in a slow oven until set.

Mrs. Mary Randolph

Tansy Pudding

Beat 6 eggs until light. Add 1 pint of cream, 1 cup of spinach juice, ¼ cup of juice of tansy. Add 1 cup of sifted cracker crumbs, 1 wineglass of wine, a dash of grated nutmeg, a pinch of salt, and sugar to taste. Stir over a low flame until it thickens. Pour into a baking dish lined with pastry and bake until set. It may be fried like an omelette.

Mrs. Mary Randolph

Ground Rice Pudding

Mix 3 tablespoonfuls of ground rice with ½ cup of cold milk. Stir it into 4 cups of scalding milk. Let it simmer for twenty minutes, stirring constantly. When cold, add 4 eggs, the juice of 1 lemon, and sugar to taste. Bake one hour. Line the dish with pastry, or not. *Mrs. Putnam*

Arrowroot Pudding

Mix 1 tablespoonful of arrowroot with 2 tablespoonfuls of cold milk. Pour into 2 cups of boiling milk. Add ⅔ cup of sugar and stir constantly. Add a dash of mace or any other flavoring, and 4 well-beaten eggs. Pour into a baking dish lined with pastry and bake until set. If it is preferred to look clear, substitute water for milk and add one more egg. *Mrs. Putnam*

Pineapple Pudding

Peel the pineapple, taking care to get all the specks out, and grate it. Take its weight in sugar and half its weight in butter. Rub the butter and sugar to a cream and stir them into the pineapple. Add 5 well-beaten eggs and 1 cup of cream. It may be baked with or without the pastry crust. *Mrs. Putnam*

Grated Apple Pudding

Pare 8 apples and put in water. Cream ½ cup butter, add ¼ cup sugar and mix well. Stir in the juice and rind of 1 lemon. Grate the apples into this mixture. Add 5 well-beaten eggs and 1 cup of milk. Bake with or without a puff paste lining the dish.

Annette

Plain Lemon Pudding

Mix juice and grated rind of 2 lemons with 2 cups of water and 2 cups of sugar. Add 2 well-beaten eggs, a pinch of salt, and 6 soda crackers, rolled to fine crumbs. Turn into dish and bake until set.

A Good Pudding

Line a baking dish with slices of bread that have been dipped in milk. Fill the dish with sliced apples, mixed with sugar and spice to taste. Cover with slices of bread soaked in milk. Set a cover on dish and bake one and one-half hours in a slow oven.

Tapioca Pudding

Put a cupful of tapioca and ½ teaspoonful of salt into 1 pint of water and let stand overnight. Peel 6 apples, core, and put in a pudding dish. Fill the centers with sugar mixed with a little nutmeg or lemon peel. Add 1 cup of water and bake one hour, turning to prevent drying. When the apples are quite soft pour over them the tapioca and bake one hour. Serve with hard sauce and cream.

Delmonico Pudding

Mix 3 tablespoonfuls of cornstarch with a little cold milk. Stir into 1 quart of hot milk, bring to a boil, and boil over a low fire for three minutes. Separate 5 eggs. Beat the yolks with 6 tablespoonfuls of sugar. Pour first mixture into this and bring to a boil. Flavor with vanilla, a pinch of salt, and strain into a pudding dish. Bake until firm. Beat the whites of the eggs to a stiff froth. Add gradually 3 tablespoonfuls of sugar and ½ teaspoonful of lemon juice. Drop into the custard from the end of a spoon, in the shape of kisses. Put in the oven until light brown. Serve cold.

A Plain Pudding

Peel 6 tart apples and grate them into a dish. Add an equal quantity of stale bread, grated. Beat 2 eggs, add 2 cups milk and 3 tablespoonfuls of sugar, dash of salt, and flavor with grated lemon or orange peel. Pour on the first mixture, stir well, and bake until set.   *Annette*

Fruit Pudding

Mix 1 cup of seeded raisins, 1 cup of currants, 1 cup of chopped suet, 1 cup sour milk, 1 teaspoonful of soda dissolved in 1 tablespoonful of hot water, ½ cup of molasses, 3 cups of flour, mixed with 1 teaspoonful of allspice, 1 of cloves, 1 of salt. Turn into a mould and boil three hours.

A Very Nice Sauce

Cream ½ cup of butter with 1 cup of powdered sugar. Beat until light. Add 1 wineglass of hot wine with a dash of nutmeg. Serve at once.   *Mrs. Annie Trist*

A Simple Batter Pudding

To 1 quart of boiling milk add 4 tablespoonfuls of Indian (corn) meal, and a pinch of salt. Simmer ten minutes. Beat 4 eggs until light and fold into first mixture. Bake until set in a slow oven, about one hour. Serve with sauce.

Mrs. Annie Trist

Sauce

Cream ½ cup of butter. Add gradually 1 cup of sugar, 1 teaspoonful of flour, 1 beaten egg, 1½ wineglasses of white wine. Just before serving add ⅔ cup of scalding milk. Bring to a boil, stirring constantly, and strain into serving dish.

Pudding Sauce

Cream ½ cup butter. Add 2 cups of brown sugar. Beat well together. Add ¼ cup of wine and ¼ cup of water. Put in saucepan and bring to a boil. Serve at once. Take care not to have it over the fire too long.

Ellen Randolph Coolidge

Quince Pudding

Peel 6 quinces, cut in pieces, cover with water and stew until soft, adding a little lemon peel. When tender, rub through a sieve, let cool, and add sugar until very sweet. Season with mace and stir in a pint of cream. Bake until set in a pie plate lined with pastry. *Mrs. Lea*

A Preserve Pudding

Take a deep baking dish, butter well and spread with a layer of preserves, either quinces, citron, apples, or peaches. Cream 1 cup of butter, add gradually 1 cup of sugar and the well-beaten yolks of 6 eggs. Pour this on the preserves and bake one-half hour. Beat the whites of the eggs, add gradually 6 tablespoonfuls of sugar. Season with currant jelly and spread over the pudding, cold, just before it goes to the table. This makes a rich dish, and is eaten without sauce. *Mrs. Lea*

Sweet Potato Pudding

Boil some sweet potatoes, peel and put through a sieve. To 2 cups of potato pulp add 1 cup of butter. Beat 6 eggs, add ¾ cup of sugar, a little nutmeg and a pinch of salt. Mix all together and bake in a pudding dish, with or without being lined with pastry until set. *Mrs. Lea*

Huckleberry Pudding

Beat 5 eggs, add 4 cups of milk and 3 tablespoonfuls of butter. Pick over 1 pint of huckleberries and roll in flour. Add to the custard, with a pinch of salt and 6 tablespoonfuls of sugar. Bake until set. *Mrs. Lea*

Macaroni Pudding

Cook macaroni in milk until tender; 2 ounces to a pint of milk will make a good-sized pudding. Add 5 eggs, ¾ cup of sugar, flavor with lemon or rose water and bake one hour. *Mrs. Horace Mann*

Sliced Apple Pudding

Beat 5 eggs very light. Add 1 pint of milk. Pare 3 apples, or 5 peaches, very thin and lay in a baking dish. Add enough flour to the milk and eggs to make a medium thick batter. Add a pinch of salt and 3 tablespoonfuls of melted butter. Pour over the fruit and bake until set. Serve with sugar, melted butter and nutmeg.

Mrs. Mary Randolph

Cocoanut Pudding

Grate a cocoanut very fine. To the cocoanut milk add 2 cups of cream, as much sugar as the cocoanut by weight, 5 well-beaten eggs and the grated rind of a lemon. Line a baking dish with pastry, pour in the cocoanut mixture, and bake one hour. It may be necessary to cover it with paper when partly baked. *Mrs. Horace Mann*

Bird's-nest Pudding

Wash and core 6 apples. Butter a dish and lay them in. Fill the cores with sugar, mixed with orange or lemon peel, or mace. Pour over them a custard or a thin batter. Bake one hour. Serve with cold sauce. *Mrs. Horace Mann*

Puddings

To be made either in a mould, tart dish, tin cake pan, or glass baking dish.

Butter well any one of these vessels. Fill lightly with the following ingredients: Either stale buns, muffins, crumpets, sliced pastry, white or brown bread sliced and buttered, the remains of sponge cakes, macaroons, almond cake, gingerbread, biscuits of any kind previously soaked. For a change with any of the above you may intermix with either fresh or dried fruits, or preserves, even plums, grated cocoanut, etc.

When the mould is full of any of the above put into a bowl ¼ teaspoonful of either ginger, cinnamon, or mixed spices, or lemon or orange peel. Beat 4 eggs. Add 4 tablespoonfuls of sugar, a pinch of salt and 3 cups of milk. Fill the pudding dish nearly to the rim. It can be either baked, boiled, or set in a saucepan ⅓ full of water, with the lid over, and let simmer for an hour, or until set. Run a knife around the edge of the dish and turn out the pudding. Pour over melted butter mixed with some sugar and the juice of a lemon, or serve with brandy sauce.   *Soyer*

Fruit Pudding

Line a baking dish with pastry. Put 1 cup of gooseberries in the bottom and cover with a generous layer of sugar, another cup of gooseberries and more sugar. Cover with pastry, tie in a cloth and drop into boiling water. Fruit puddings, such as apple or rhubarb, are made in the same manner. Boil one hour. Remove from saucepan, untie cloth, turn pudding out on a dish and serve with sugar sprinkled over it and cream. Ripe cherries, currants, raspberries, greengage plums and such like fruit will not require as much sugar or so long boiling.   *Soyer*

Curd Milk Pudding

Mix 2 cups of curds (cottage cheese) with 3 well-beaten eggs, ½ teaspoonful of grated lemon peel, 4 tablespoonfuls of currants, ¼ teaspoonful of salt, ¾ cup of sugar and 2 cups of bread crumbs. Mix well. Turn into a pudding cloth that has been rinsed in cold water and dusted with flour. Boil ¾ of an hour. Serve with any desired sauce.   *Soyer*

Cocoanut Pudding

Grate ½ cocoanut. Add 1 well beaten egg to the milk of the cocoanut, mix both together. Add 2 tablespoonfuls of flour, a pinch of salt and sugar to taste. Bake until set. *Soyer*

Ground Rice Pudding

Bring 2 cups of milk to a boil with a piece of lemon peel. Mix ½ cup of ground rice with 1 cup of milk, 4 tablespoonfuls of sugar, 1 tablespoonful of melted butter and a pinch of salt. Add to hot milk. Keep stirring. Remove from fire, add 2 beaten eggs, stir well. Butter a pie dish, pour in the mixture, and bake until set. This is one of the quickest puddings that can be made.   *Soyer*

Handy Pudding

Mix 1 cup of sugar with the juice of 3 lemons. Roll a strip of pastry as for roly-poly pudding, about 14 inches long and 10 inches wide. Spread the mixture over this with a spoon. Roll, put in a pudding cloth that has been wrung out of water and dusted with flour. Boil the same as roly-poly pudding. Serve with any desired sauce.

Orange can be done the same way, with the addition of the juice of ½ lemon.   *Soyer*

Cold Sauce

Cream 1 cup of butter. Add ½ cup of sugar and stir well
until very light. Add the juice and grated rind of 1 lemon,
and any additional flavor desired.   *Mrs. Putnam*

Charlotte

Stew any desired fruit until soft. Sweeten to taste and
put in any spices you may wish. There should be 2 cups.
Trim the crusts of slices of bread and cut bread to about
the width of two fingers. Dip in batter and fry until a
golden brown. Powder with sugar. Butter a round baking
pan or pyrex dish and line with the fingers of fried bread.
Pour the fruit in and set in a moderate oven for half an
hour. Turn out on a platter. Set under the broiler a moment to glaze the sugar.   *Monticello*

Pancakes

Sift 2 cups of flour into a bowl with a pinch of salt. Beat
the yolks of 5 eggs, add 2 tablespoonfuls of cooking oil to
them and stir into flour. Add cream until the batter is very
thin. Beat the whites of 3 eggs very stiff and mix with the
batter. Put a tablespoonful of butter in a small iron skillet, pour in a thin layer of batter. Fry a little brown, turn,
and brown other side. Sprinkle with sugar as you lay
them on the dish. The top one should be glazed under
the broiler. A little lemon juice, currants or raisins mixed
into the batter is an improvement.

In serving, turn a plate bottom upwards, lay the pancakes upon it. You cut through all, in serving them, like a
pie or a cake.   *Lemaire*

CREAMS

Burnt Cream

Bring 4 cups of milk to a boil with a large piece of orange peel; beat the yolks of 6 eggs and the whites of 2 until light, add gradually 6 tablespoonfuls of sugar that have been mixed with 2 tablespoonfuls of flour and a pinch of salt, stir this gradually into the milk and continue stirring until thick; add 1 tablespoonful of butter and strain through a sieve into a deep baking dish. Sift a layer of powdered sugar, about one-half of an inch thick over the cream and put under a broiler until glazed. Serve very cold. It is usual to season it with essence of lemon, mixed with the sugar, or anything else you prefer to flavor it with.

Julien, Thomas Jefferson's French cook in Washington

Snow Eggs

Separate 5 eggs and beat the whites until you can turn the vessel bottom upwards without their leaving it. Gradually add 1 tablespoonful of powdered sugar and ½ teaspoonful of any desired flavoring (Jefferson used orange flower or rose water).

Put 2 cups of milk into a saucepan, add 3 tablespoonfuls of sugar, flavoring, and bring slowly to a boil. Drop the first mixture into the milk and poach until well set. Lay them on a wire drainer to drain.

Beat the yolk of 1 egg until thick, stir gradually into the milk. Add a pinch of salt. As soon as the custard thickens pour through a sieve. Put your whites in a serving dish and pour the custard over them. A little wine stirred in is a great improvement. *James, cook at Monticello*

Chocolate Cream

Shave 2 squares of chocolate, add ¼ cup water and stir until melted. Add 4 cups milk, dash of salt, 6 tablespoonfuls of sugar, 1 teaspoonful of vanilla, and heat until lukewarm. Dissolve 2 junket tablets in 2 tablespoonfuls of cold water, stir gently into first mixture and pour into moulds. Let stand one-half hour, then set in refrigerator.

Tea Creams

If the creams are to be made with tea, pour the milk boiling on the tea and let it draw. Let cool until lukewarm, strain and proceed as in the foregoing. Omit all other flavoring.

Coffee Creams

If with coffee the same, observing to pour the milk hot on
the coffee and not to cook the grains.   *James*

Plain Custard No. 1

To 4 cups of milk add a piece of stick cinnamon and heat
to the scalding point. Let cool. Beat the yolks of 5, 8 or 12
eggs, according to the richness you wish to give your
custard (some people put in some of the whites) with 6
tablespoonfuls of sugar and a pinch of salt, and add to the
milk. Add a glass of white wine and pass through a sieve.
Pour into custard cups, set in a pan of cold water, and
bake in a slow oven until set. This may be determined by
running a silver knife through.   *Mrs. Martha Randolph*

Italian Cream

Mix 1 pint cream, 1 cupful of white wine, the juice of
2 lemons, and 6 tablespoonfuls of sugar. Soak 2 scant
tablespoonfuls of gelatine in ¼ cup water. Dissolve in
½ cup boiling water. Add to first mixture. Strain into
moulds and let stand until set.   *Mrs. Martha Randolph*

Floating Island

Beat the whites of 3 eggs until stiff. Add ½ cupful of jelly,
3 tablespoonfuls of syrup, or whatever you choose to season it with, add sugar to taste. Lay this in spoonfuls upon
a bowl of rich milk, with wine, sugar to taste, and any
fruit of the season.   *Mrs. Martha Randolph*

Sago Cream

Bring 2 cups of milk to a boil. Add gradually 2 table-spoonfuls of sago and cook until clear, stirring constantly. Beat the yolk of 1 egg until light, add to it 3 tablespoonfuls of sugar, ½ cup of cream, a pinch of salt, and a few grains of mace. Add to first mixture and set over a low fire until thick, taking care it does not curdle. When cold, season to taste with wine and serve up in glasses.

Mrs. Martha Randolph

Cream Cheese

Put 1 quart of cream in a stone jar and keep it there until it forms a curd. Put a cheesecloth over a bowl and lay the curd on it to drain for twenty-four hours. Add salt to taste. Beat the curd well and form into pats like butter. It requires a week or ten days to ripen.

The remains of breakfast cream put in the stone jar each day answer as well as any other to make this cheese.

Lemaire, Thomas Jefferson's steward in Washington

Ice Cream

Scald 1 quart of cream. Beat the yolks of 6 eggs with 1 cupful of sugar. Pour gradually into the milk and stir until thick. Add a pinch of salt, stir well, and strain into a bowl. Add 1 tablespoonful of vanilla and turn into a freezer. Surround with a mixture of 3 parts ice to 1 part of salt. Turn handle of freezer until mixture is thick. Pack into mould, surround with ice and salt—one measure of salt to four of ice, and let stand until set.

If you have not cream, fresh butter creamed and mixed with the milk, ¼ cupful to 4 cups of milk, will answer very well, as also to make fruit ices. *Petit*

Soft Custard

Scald 1 quart of milk, partly cream if you have it. Pour onto from 6 to 12 well-beaten eggs, according to richness desired. Strain, and bring to boiling point. Add 7 table-spoonfuls of sugar, and any flavoring desired.   *Mrs. Allen*

Raspberry or Strawberry Ice Cream

If you cannot procure rich cream, make a quart of rich boiled custard. When cold, pour it on a quart of ripe strawberries or raspberries that have been well mashed. Pass through a fine sieve, sweeten to taste, add a pinch of salt and one teaspoonful of vanilla. Freeze.

(Monticello) Mrs. Mary Randolph

Peach Cream

Take a dozen fine, ripe peaches, peel them, remove the stones and put them in a china bowl. Sprinkle 1 cupful of sugar on them and chop them very small with a silver spoon. If the peaches are sufficiently ripe they will become a smooth pulp. Add as much cream as you have peaches. Add more sugar (if necessary), a pinch of salt and ½ teaspoonful of almond extract. Freeze.

(Monticello) Mrs. Mary Randolph

Citron Cream

Cut the finest citron melons when perfectly ripe, remove the seeds, and slice the nicest part into a china bowl, in small pieces that will lie conveniently. Cover them with powdered sugar and let stand for several hours. Then drain off the syrup they have made, add as much cream as it will give a strong flavor to, and freeze it.

Pineapple Cream

This is made the same way as citron cream.

Mrs. Mary Randolph

Lemon Cream

Pare the yellow rind very thin from 4 lemons, put it in a quart of thin cream and bring to a boil. Squeeze and strain the juice of one lemon, saturate it completely with powdered sugar. When the cream is quite cold, stir it very slowly into the lemon and sugar mixture, taking care that it does not curdle. If not sufficiently sweet, add more sugar, also a pinch of salt. Freeze. *Mrs. Mary Randolph*

Lemonade Iced

Make a quart of rich lemonade. (Boil 1 quart of water with 2 cups of sugar for twelve minutes. Add ⅔ cup of lemon juice, strain and cool.) Beat the whites of 6 eggs to a stiff froth. Add a pinch of salt. Stir the lemonade into this thoroughly. Freeze.

Other Fruits

The juice of cherries or of currants mixed with water and sugar and prepared in the same manner, make very delicate ices.

Mrs. Mary Randolph

Iced Jelly

Make a wine jelly, not very thick, freeze it and serve it in glasses. For the jelly, soak 1 tablespoonful of gelatine in ¼ cup water for five minutes. Dissolve in 1½ cups of boiling water. Add 1 cup sugar, 1 cup sherry or Madeira wine, ⅓ cup orange juice, 3 tablespoonfuls of lemon juice.

Chocolate Cream

Scrape ¼ pound chocolate very fine. Add 3 tablespoonfuls of water and stir over a low flame until melted. Add 4 cups of scalded milk. Beat the yolks of 6 eggs until light, add 6 tablespoonfuls of sugar and a pinch of salt. Pour into first mixture and stir until it thickens. Add 1 teaspoonful of vanilla. Strain into a glass dish.

(Monticello) Mrs. Mary Randolph

Coffee Cream

Scald 2 cups of milk with 2 tablespoonfuls of ground coffee. Strain through a fine cheesecloth or napkin. Beat the yolks of 4 eggs with 4 tablespoonfuls of sugar, add to the milk and stir over a low flame until thick. Add 1 teaspoonful of vanilla and strain into a glass dish.

(Monticello) Mrs. Mary Randolph

Custard No. 3

Scald 1 quart of milk and let stand until cool. Beat 6 eggs slightly with ¾ cup of sugar and a pinch of salt. Add to milk, strain into custard cups. Set in a pan of water and bake in a slow oven until set. Grate nutmeg on top when cold. Serve them in the cups with the covers on, and a teaspoon on the dish between each cup.   *Mrs. Mary Randolph*

Trifle

Put slices of savory (sponge) cake or Naples' biscuit in the bottom of a deep dish. Moisten well with white wine and fill the dish nearly to the top with rich, boiled custard. Season half a pint of thick cream with white wine and sugar, whip it to a froth. As it rises take it lightly off with a silver spoon and lay it on the custard. Pile it up high and tastily. Decorate it with preserves of any kind, cut it so thin as not to bear the froth down by its weight.

Mrs. Mary Randolph

Floating Island

Have the bowl nearly full of syllabub made by mixing 3 cups of rich milk with sugar and white wine to taste. Beat the whites of 4 eggs until very stiff and mix with them raspberry or strawberry marmalade, enough to flavor and color it. Lay the froth lightly on the syllabub, first putting in some slices of cake. Raise it in little mounds and garnish with something light.   *Mrs. Mary Randolph*

Tea Cream

Put 1 tablespoonful of best tea in a pitcher and pour on it 1 tablespoonful of water. Let it stand an hour to soften the leaves. Then pour over it 2 cups of cream that has been brought to a boil, cover close, and let stand half an hour. Strain. Add 3 tablespoonfuls of sugar. Dissolve one junket tablet in a tablespoonful of cold water. When the cream is lukewarm, add the junket. Pour into glasses and let stand until set.   *Mrs. Mary Randolph*

Syllabub

Season 2 cups of rich milk with sugar and white wine to taste, but not enough to curdle it. Fill glasses nearly full and crown them with whipped cream seasoned.

Mrs. Mary Randolph

Gooseberry Fool

Pick the stems and blossoms off 1 quart of gooseberries, put them in a saucepan with their weight in sugar and 2 tablespoonfuls of water. Stew slowly for forty minutes. Press through a fine sieve and when cold add rich custard until it is the consistency of thick cream. Put it in a glass bowl and lay whipped cream on top.   *Mrs. Mary Randolph*

Almond Custard

Blanch ¼ pound of almonds and put them through the food chopper, using finest grinder. Put them in 4 cups of milk and bring to boiling point. Beat 6 eggs with 6 table-spoonfuls of sugar and a pinch of salt. Pour milk on them, put in double boiler and stir until the custard has thickened.   *Mrs. Horace Mann*

Slip

Heat 2 cups of milk until lukewarm. Dissolve 1 junket tablet in 1 tablespoonful of cold water and stir into the milk. Let stand until cold, when it will be as stiff as jelly. Set it on ice. It must be eaten with powdered sugar, cream and nutmeg.   *Mrs. Mary Randolph*

Curds and Cream

Prepare 4 cups of milk as for slip. Let stand until just before it is to be served. Then take it up with a skimmer and lay on a sieve. When the whey has drained off put the curds in a dish and surround them with cream. Serve with sugar and nutmeg.   *Mrs. Mary Randolph*

Whip

Mix 1 cupful of sugar with the juice of 3 lemons. Add 1 pint of heavy cream and whip until stiff. Serve in glasses. Pineapple juice adds to the goodness.   *Mrs. Horace Mann*

Whip for Garnishing

Sweeten heavy cream and flavor it to taste. Set on ice and when very cold whip until the foam rises.

A spoonful of jam or jelly in the bottom of a glass, covered with whip is a tasteful dish for dessert, or for an evening party.

If you wish to color the whip, a few spoonfuls of fruit juice will do it.   *Mrs. Horace Mann*

Kiss Froth

Beat the white of an egg to a stiff froth. Sift on a very little sugar and set in the oven to brown slightly. It makes a very pretty garnishing for sweet dishes. *Mrs. Horace Mann*

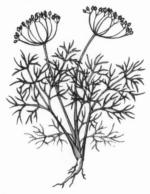

Flavoring

A quart of raspberries or strawberries will flavor a gallon of cream.

A common-sized pineapple, sliced, sugared and strained, after standing all night, *ditto.*

Rub lumps of sugar over the outsides of three lemons, squeeze them, strain the juice, and add as much sugar as will absorb it, to flavor one gallon of cream.

Mrs. Horace Mann

Apple Cream

Core 6 apples and bake them. When done, remove skins. Separate 2 eggs, beat the yolks and add to the apple pulp. Sweeten to taste and beat vigorously for fifteen minutes. Put in a dish. Beat the whites of the eggs until stiff, add gradually 3 tablespoonfuls of sugar. Spread over the apple mixture and sift a little powdered sugar over all.

Snow Rice Cream

Put in a stewpan 4 ounces ground rice, 6 tablespoonfuls of sugar, 3 tablespoonfuls of butter, a pinch of salt, ½ teaspoonful of almond extract, or any preferred flavor, and 1 quart of milk. Bring to a boil and cook gently until it forms a smooth substance, though not too thick, about fifteen to twenty minutes.

Pour it into a buttered mould and serve when cold. It will turn out like jelly.

The rice had better be done a little too much, than under.

Soyer

Bohemian Cream

Take any preferred stewed fruit, such as apricots, strawberries or peaches, and pass them through a sieve. There should be one cupful. Soak 1 tablespoonful of gelatine in ½ cup of water for five minutes and dissolve in ½ cup boiling water. Add to the fruit. Whip 1 pint of cream and add gradually to fruit pulp. Add pinch of salt. Turn into a mould and let set on ice until firm.

Soyer

White Cream

Put into a basin 3 tablespoonfuls of sugar, ¼ cup brandy, and 1 tablespoonful of gelatine, which has been soaked in 2 tablespoonfuls of water for five minutes. Then dissolve in ½ cup boiling water. Stir well. Add 1 pint of cream, whipped, and turn into a mould. Rum, Curaçoa, or other liqueurs or flavors may be added. When liqueurs are used, add less sugar.

Soyer

Ice Cream

Scald 1 quart of milk and stir in gradually the yolks of 6 eggs which have been beaten light with a wineglassful of water and 7 tablespoonfuls of sugar. Add pinch of salt. Stir until the custard thickens. Strain into a bowl. Let cool. Add 2 teaspoonfuls of vanilla or lemon extract. Freeze.

Mrs. Louise Derby, New York

Clouted Cream

Pour 1 cupful of milk and 1 cupful of cream into a saucepan of a size so that it will be about three inches deep. Let stand for twenty-four hours. Then place it upon a slow fire so that it may gradually warm, but not boil, which would spoil it. When the cream forms a ring in the middle, put a little of it aside with the finger, and if a few bubbles rise in that spot, it is done. It will generally take from half to three-quarters of an hour. Let it stand in a cool place another twenty-four hours. Then skim it and dust a little sugar over the top of the cream.

Mrs. Horace Mann

French Receipts

Coffee, Cocoa, or Chocolate Custard

Put in a pan 1 cup of very strong coffee and 1 cup of milk. Bring to a boil. Beat 4 eggs and add 4 tablespoonfuls of sugar and a pinch of salt. Add the hot milk, stir well, and pass through a strainer. Fill custard cups with the mixture, set in a pan of water and bake until set. Chocolate and cocoa the same. *Soyer*

Custard in Pie Dish

Put a border of puff paste around the dish and fill with the above, or with plain custard. Bake half an hour in a slow oven. Serve cold. *Soyer*

Velvet Cream

Put in a dessert dish a thick layer of strawberry jam or any other preserve and put over it a pint of hot snow cream mixture. When cold the top may be ornamented with fresh or preserved fruit.   *Soyer*

Index